AGRICULTURE

THIRD EDITION

Ferguson's
An Infobase Learning Company

Careers in Focus: Agriculture, Third Edition

Copyright © 2012 by Infobase Learning

Ferguson's
An imprint of Infobase Learning
132 West 31st Street
New York NY 10001

Library of Congress Cataloging-in-Publication Data

Careers in focus. Agriculture. — 3rd ed.
    p. cm.
  Cover title: Ferguson's careers in focus. Agriculture
  Includes bibliographical references and index.
  ISBN-13: 978-0-8160-8036-6 (hardcover : alk. paper)
  ISBN-10: 0-8160-8036-4 (hardcover : alk. paper) 1. Agriculture—Vocational guidance—United States. I. Ferguson Publishing. II. Title: Agriculture. III. Title: Ferguson's careers in focus. Agriculture.
  S494.5.A4C27 2011
  630.203—dc23   2011016076

Ferguson's books are available at special discounts when purchased in bulk quantities for businesses, associations, institutions, or sales promotions. Please call our Special Sales Department in New York at (212) 967-8800 or (800) 322-8755.

You can find Ferguson's on the World Wide Web at
http://www.infobaselearning.com

Text design by David Strelecky
Composition by Erika K. Arroyo
Cover printed by Yurchak Printing, Landisville, Pa.
Book printed and bound by Yurchak Printing, Landisville, Pa.
Date printed: October 2011
Printed in the United States of America

10 9 8 7 6 5 4 3 2 1

This book is printed on acid-free paper.

Table of Contents

Introduction

The American agricultural industry is vast and diverse. It is made up of the *farmers* who cultivate the land, raise livestock, and grow plants; the industries that purchase, process, distribute, and transport farm products and farm supplies; and the organizations that supply services to the farmer and the consumer. This whole complex network of activities is often called agribusiness.

The base for all agricultural work is the farm. The average farm is run by a *farm operator* or a *farm manager*, who in most cases has attended college and earned a degree in agriculture. Farms usually employ both permanent and seasonal workers. Part-time employees work during the harvest and planting seasons, and permanent employees are responsible for the day-to-day operations of the farm throughout the year.

Single-crop farms are commonplace. On these farms, the cash crop (the crop that is grown for sale) is the only thing produced. Wheat and corn single-crop farms are widespread throughout the Midwest and Plains states. Specialized livestock production is mainly centered on cattle, hogs, and poultry operations in the United States. Sheep, goat, turkey, and aquaculture (fish, mollusks, and crustaceans) farms are examples of single-livestock operations.

Diversified farms produce several different crops or animals, or a mixture of both, for sale. The old-style family farm was often a diversified farm. These farms are less common now, partly because of the simplicity of specialized production, but mainly because the profit margin is often higher with single-crop production. Land is normally well suited to only a few types of plants or animals, which makes diversification difficult. However, the diversified farm is less dependent on the success of a single item. Drought, disease, and other natural disasters may take less of a toll on the farm that produces many different products.

Farmers depend on off-the-farm industries to provide seed, fertilizer, and machinery. After the crops are harvested or livestock are bred, output industries process and market the farm products. Storage, shipping, processing, packaging, and canning are just some of the industries that assist the farmer in the sale of goods. For example, a shipping company makes sure that a farm's produce reaches the customer in the best condition for sale. A storage company makes sure that all of a farm's apples produced in September do not arrive at the store on the same day. It will store some of the apples for future sales, schedule future deliveries, and can some produce for off-season sales. These are all important aspects of agribusiness.

To ensure sales of their produce, farmers can arrange to sell their crops before producing them. This is known as contract farming, and it has benefits for both the buyer and the farmer. It is an arrangement between a farm and a buyer, such as a food processor or marketer, to ship the produce to the buyer upon harvesting. The farmer must agree to a price at the time of the contract. If there are a lot of successful crops of the type the farmer sells, the farmer may get a higher price for the crops in a contract than if he had waited for the harvest and bid with many other farmers waiting to sell their goods. However, if crop production is low, then the buyer may get a cheaper price on a product if the buyer arranged the contract early in the season, before the farmer knew that there would be fewer of the items produced than normal. In an open sale, the farmer would be able to raise the price, because there would be more people trying to buy from him or her.

The off-the-farm portion of the agricultural industry, in addition to offering goods and services, also provides an opportunity for many diverse and interesting careers such as *food technologists, agricultural scientists, agricultural economists,* and *commodities brokers.*

Experiment stations conduct research on farming techniques to develop the most effective methods of farming for each region. Scientists at the stations work with soils, crops, feed rations, animals, plant variations, and genetic strains to devise the best farming method for the climate and the zone in which they work. Some states have several stations working in different areas to account for regional differences.

After years of decline, employment in the agricultural industry is expected to remain stable through 2018, according to the U.S. Department of Labor (DOL).

Overproduction, increasing productivity, and industry consolidation have reduced opportunities in the industry—especially for self-employed farmers—but there will continue to be openings in the field as agricultural workers retire or leave the industry for other reasons.

The DOL predicts that several trends should help farmers and other specialized agricultural workers. Some farmers are prospering by focusing on growing specialty crops, participating in farmer-owned and operated cooperatives, or switching to all-organic farming practices in response to public fears about the effects of pesticides and fertilizers used in traditional agriculture. Aquaculture will also become more important and more profitable in the next decade. Growth in aquaculture is spurred by declining ocean catches due to overfishing and the growing demand for seafood items, such as shrimp, salmon, and catfish.

Another important development in agriculture involves methods of processing grains to make new products and helping farmers to deal with crop surpluses. In many agriculture-based states, adding value to agricultural products is the largest creator of wealth and jobs. The pursuit of new uses for farm crops will provide many jobs for those involved in processing and will also provide farmers with new markets for their crops. For example, corn is used for ethanol, sweeteners, feed products, corn oil, and lactic acid. Studies are underway that will expand corn's uses to include adhesives, paper and packaging, nonprescription medical products, and even plastic.

Food safety is an important issue that will impact jobs for food scientists, agricultural scientists, and agricultural inspectors. Recent outbreaks of mad cow disease and foot-and-mouth disease in livestock in Europe have prompted heightened efforts to detect and prevent these problems in the United States. There are also concerns about the West Nile virus, anthrax, *E. coli* bacteria in livestock and meat products, and residual pesticides in plant products. Efforts are also being made to protect the industry from agroterrorism.

Genetic engineering in both plant and animal agriculture is being hotly debated in the agricultural and political communities, as well as among consumers. Some proponents of genetic engineering believe that engineering crops and livestock to be more resistant to disease, insects, and other problems and to have longer shelf lives will greatly benefit farmers. However, the effects of genetic engineering on the environment and on humans, as well as the long-term effects on the agricultural products themselves, have not yet been determined. Research, experimentation, and debate are likely to continue for decades.

Some farmers are earning additional income by dealing in renewable energy, particularly selling wind power. Others are growing crops to produce ethanol, biodiesel, and biomass, as well as generating electricity from the methane produced by livestock feeding operations.

More diverse career opportunities are available for those with advanced degrees in agriculture-related fields. Agricultural workers will see their jobs expand to involve high-tech methods of conservation, planting, tilling, and treating farm crops.

Farm managers and operators will need extensive understanding of new farming methods and equipment, as well as computer-aided operations, in order to remain competitive in this increasingly difficult segment of the job market.

Each article in *Careers in Focus: Agriculture* discusses a particular agricultural career in detail. Many of the articles in the book appear in Ferguson's *Encyclopedia of Careers and Vocational Guidance,* but have been updated and revised with the latest information from the DOL and other sources. This edition of the book also contains new articles on *agricultural economists, farmers' market managers and promoters,* and *organic farmers.*

The **Quick Facts** section provides a brief summary of the career, including recommended school subjects, personal skills, work environment, minimum educational requirements, salary ranges, certification or licensing requirements, and employment outlook. This section also provides acronyms and identification numbers for the following government classification indexes: the Dictionary of Occupational Titles (DOT), the Guide for Occupational Exploration (GOE), the National Occupational Classification (NOC) Index, and the Occupational Information Network (O*NET)-Standard Occupational Classification System (SOC) index. The DOT, GOE, and O*NET-SOC indexes have been created by the U.S. government; the NOC index is Canada's career classification system. Readers can use the identification numbers listed in the Quick Facts section to access further information about a career. Print editions of the DOT (*Dictionary of Occupational Titles.* Indianapolis, Ind.: JIST Works, 1991) and GOE (*Guide for Occupational Exploration.* Indianapolis, Ind.: JIST Works, 2001) are available at libraries. Electronic versions of the DOT (http://www.oalj.dol.gov/libdot.htm), NOC (http://www5.hrsdc.gc.ca/NOC), and O*NET-SOC (http://www.onetonline.org) are available on the Internet. When no DOT, GOE, NOC, or O*NET-SOC numbers are listed, this means that the U.S. Department of Labor or Human Resources and Skills Development Canada have not created a numerical designation for this career. In this instance, you will see the acronym "N/A," or not available.

The **Overview** section is a brief introductory description of the duties and responsibilities involved in this career. Oftentimes, a career may have a variety of job titles. When this is the case, alternative career titles are presented. Employment statistics are also provided, when available. The **History** section describes the history of the particular job as it relates to the overall development of its industry or field. **The Job** describes the primary and secondary duties of the job. **Requirements** discusses high school and postsecondary education and training requirements, any certification or licensing that is necessary, and other personal requirements for success in the job. **Exploring** offers suggestions on how to gain experience in or knowledge of the particular job before making a firm educational and financial commitment. The focus is on what can be done while still in high school (or in the early years of college) to gain a better understanding of the job. The **Employers** section gives an overview of typical places of employment for the job. **Starting Out** discusses the best ways to land that first job, be it through the college career services office, newspaper ads, Internet employment sites, or personal contact. The **Advancement** section describes what kind of career path to expect from the job and how to get there. **Earnings** lists salary ranges and describes the typical fringe benefits. The **Work Environment** section describes the typical surroundings and conditions of employment—whether indoors or outdoors, noisy or quiet, social or independent. Also discussed are typical hours worked, any seasonal fluctuations, and the stresses and strains of the job. The **Outlook** section summarizes the job in terms of the general economy and industry projections. For the most part, Outlook information is obtained from the U.S. Bureau of Labor Statistics and is supplemented by information gathered from professional associations. Job growth terms follow those used in the *Occupational Outlook Handbook*. Growth described as "much faster than the average" means an increase of 20 percent or more. Growth described as "faster than the average" means an increase of 14 to 19 percent. Growth described as "about as fast as the average" means an increase of 7 to 13 percent. Growth described as "more slowly than the average" means an increase of 3 to 6 percent. "Little or no change" means a decrease of 2 percent to an increase of 2 percent. "Decline" means a decrease of 3 percent or more. Each article ends with **For More Information,** which lists organizations that provide information on training, education, internships, scholarships, and job placement.

Careers in Focus: Agriculture also includes photographs, informative sidebars, and interviews with professionals in the field.

Agribusiness Technicians

QUICK FACTS

School Subjects
Agriculture
Business

Personal Skills
Leadership/management
Technical/scientific

Work Environment
Indoors and outdoors
Primarily multiple locations

Minimum Education Level
Associate's degree

Salary Range
$22,010 to $44,180 to
$73,400+

Certification or Licensing
None available

Outlook
Little or no change

DOT
N/A

GOE
12.03.02

NOC
N/A

O*NET-SOC
25-9021.00

OVERVIEW

Agribusiness technicians combine their agriculture and business backgrounds to manage or offer management consulting services to farms and agricultural businesses. Agribusiness technicians, also called *agricultural business technicians,* generally work as liaisons between farms and agricultural businesses, representing either the farm or the business.

HISTORY

The marketing of agricultural products first concerned farmers in the early 20th century. Cooperative organizations were formed in the 1920s, allowing farmers to control the marketing of their commodities, but farmers still struggled to make profits. It was about this time that the field of agricultural economics evolved; the International Association of Agricultural Economics was established in 1929.

The Dust Bowl of the 1930s complicated farm economics further, leading to New Deal legislation. Under the New Deal, which enacted the first effective farm legislation in the United States, the secretary of agriculture could control crop production. In the following years, agriculture expanded as a result of scientific advances and better methods of planting and harvesting. By the 1960s, marketing had become much more complicated for farmers, leading to the development of agribusiness as a major career field. Today, agribusiness is much larger than the farming industry; two-thirds of each dollar spent on food goes toward processing, packaging, marketing, and retailing, with only one-third going to the farm.

6

Inside the U.S. Department of Agriculture (USDA)

Professionals and technicians with agricultural education and training can find work with a number of USDA agencies, including the following:

- Agricultural Research Service (ARS, http://www.ars.usda.gov): The principal in-house research agency of the USDA.
- National Agricultural Library (http://www.nalusda.gov): Part of the ARS; a major international source for agriculture information; one of four national libraries in the country.
- Economic Research Service (http://www.ers.usda.gov): Provides information about agriculture and natural resources.
- National Agricultural Statistics Service (http://www.nass.usda. gov): Administers the USDA's program for collecting and publishing timely national and state agricultural statistics.

THE JOB

Agribusiness is as diverse a field as agriculture, and it involves professionals in economics, sales, marketing, commodities, science, and other areas. Technicians assist these professionals. They may work for a farm or for a business or organization that assists farmers. They may spend their workdays out in the field or behind a desk or a combination of these two. Their work may focus on such areas as grain, livestock, or dairy farm production.

Some agribusiness technicians choose to go into business management, working as part of a personnel-management office for a large corporate farm or dairy. In such a position, the technician manages staff, coordinates work plans with farm managers, and oversees the entire salary structure for farm or other production workers. Other agribusiness technicians work as *purchasing agents,* supervising all the buying for large commercial farms. Another option for the agribusiness technician is to work as a *farm sales representative,* finding the best markets for the produce of farms on a local, state, or national level. In this capacity, the technician travels a great deal and works closely with records technicians and other personnel of the farm or farms he or she represents.

Some agribusiness technicians assist farmers with record keeping. The records that farmers and other agricultural business people must keep are becoming more detailed and varied every year. Agribusiness technicians may set up complete record-keeping systems. They analyze records and help farmers make management decisions based on the accumulated facts. Computerized record keeping is common now, so there is a tremendous need for *agricultural records technicians* who can create tailor-made programs to help farmers get maximum benefit from their output. Furthermore, they analyze the output and make practical applications of the information.

In some positions, such as *agricultural quality control technician,* the technician works directly with farmers but is employed by another company. *Dairy production field-contact technicians,* for example, serve as contact people between dairy companies and the farms that produce the milk. They negotiate long- or short-term contracts to purchase milk and milk products according to agreed specifications; meet with farmers to test milk for butterfat content, sediment, and bacteria; and discuss ways to solve milk-production problems and improve production. They may suggest methods of feeding, housing, and milking to improve production or comply with sanitary regulations. They may set up truck routes to haul milk to the dairy; solicit membership in cooperative associations; or even sell items such as dairy-farm equipment, chemicals, and feed to the farmers they contact.

Poultry field-service technicians represent food-processing companies or cooperative associations. They inspect farms to ensure compliance with agreements involving facilities, equipment, sanitation, and efficiency. They also advise farmers on how to improve the quality of their products. Technicians may examine chickens for evidence of disease and growth rate to determine the effectiveness of medication and feeding programs. They may then recommend changes in equipment or procedures to improve production. They inform farmers of new techniques, government regulations, and company or association production standards so they can upgrade their farms to meet requirements. They may recommend laboratory testing of feeds, diseased chickens, and diet supplements. In these cases, they often gather samples and take them to a laboratory for analysis. They report their findings on farm conditions, laboratory tests, their own recommendations, and farmers' reactions to the company or association employing them.

Agribusiness technicians also work for credit institutions that solicit the business of farmers, make appraisals of real estate and personal property, organize and present loan requests, close loans, and service those loans with periodic reviews of the borrower's management performance and financial status. They also work as farm representatives for banks, cooperatives, or federal lending institutions. In this capacity they sell their organizations' services to farmers or agricultural business people, make appraisals, and do the paperwork involved with lending money.

REQUIREMENTS

High School

In high school, you should take social studies, laboratory science (biology, chemistry, and physics), mathematics, and, if possible, agriculture and business classes. English and composition will be particularly helpful, since oral and written communications are central to the work of the agribusiness technician. Also, take computer classes so that you are familiar with using this technology. Computers are often used in record keeping and production planning.

Postsecondary Training

After completing high school, it is necessary to train in a two-year agricultural or technical college. Many colleges offer associate's degrees in agribusiness or agricultural management. The programs concentrate on basic economic theory; training in management analysis and practical problem solving; and intensive communications training, such as public speaking and report writing.

Typical first-year courses in an agricultural or technical college include English, biology, health and physical education, introductory animal husbandry, principles of accounting, agricultural economics, microbiology, botany, introductory data processing, soil science, and principles of business.

Typical second-year courses include marketing agricultural commodities, farm management, social science, agricultural finance, agricultural marketing institutions, forage and seed crops, personnel management, and agricultural records and taxation.

Other Requirements

You must be able to work well with other people; this includes being able to delegate responsibility and establish friendly relations with farmers, laborers, and company managers. You must be able to analyze management problems and make sound decisions based on your analysis. And you must have excellent oral and written communication skills. Technicians are expected to present written and oral reports, offer comments and advice clearly, and, when necessary, train other workers for a particular job.

EXPLORING

Try to get summer or part-time employment in your desired specialty—for example, a clerical job in a farm insurance agency or as a laborer in a feed and grain company. Because many technical colleges offer evening courses, it may be possible to obtain permission during your senior year to audit a course or even to take it for future college credit. Work experience on a farm will give you insight into the business concerns of farmers, as will industry periodicals such as *Farm Journal* (http://www.agweb.com/farmjournal) and *Grain Journal* (http://www.grainnet.com). Join your high school's chapter of the National FFA Organization (formerly known as Future Farmers of America) or a local 4-H group, where you may have the opportunity to work on farm-management projects.

EMPLOYERS

Many different agriculture-based businesses hire graduates of agribusiness programs. Employers include large commercial farms, grain elevators, credit unions, farm equipment dealerships, farm supply stores, fertilizer and processing plants, agricultural chemical companies, and local, state, and federal government agencies.

STARTING OUT

Your agribusiness program will likely require a semester or more of employment experience and will assist you in finding an internship or part-time job with agribusiness professionals. Many students are able to turn their internships into full-time work or make connections that lead to other job opportunities. Most agribusiness technician jobs are considered entry-level, or management trainee, positions and don't require a great deal of previous experience. These jobs are often advertised in the classifieds or posted with career services offices at community colleges.

ADVANCEMENT

The ultimate aim of many technicians is to own their own business. Technicians can start their own companies in any agricultural business area or act as *freelance agents* under contract to perform specific services for several firms. For example, an experienced agribusiness technician may purchase a computer and data-processing software, set up the necessary record-keeping programs, and act as a consulting firm for a host of farms and agricultural businesses.

There are many other positions an agribusiness technician may hold. *Farm managers* oversee all operations of a farm and work closely with owners and other management, customers, and all farm departments on larger farms. *Regional farm credit managers* supervise several of a bank's farm representatives. They may suggest training programs for farm representatives, recommend changes in lending procedures, and conduct personal audits of randomly selected farm accounts. *Sales managers* act as liaisons between company sales representatives and individual dealers, distributors, or farmers.

EARNINGS

The U.S. Department of Labor (DOL) reports that agribusiness technicians who provide management and technical consulting services earned median annual salaries of $44,180 in 2009. Ten percent of all such farm and home advisers earned less than $22,010, and 10 percent earned $73,400 or more a year.

Fringe benefits vary widely, depending upon the employer. Some amount to as much as one-third of the base salary. More and more employers are providing such benefits as pension plans, paid vacations, insurance, and tuition reimbursement.

WORK ENVIRONMENT

Because the field is so large, working environments may be anywhere from a corporate office to a cornfield. Those who work in sales are likely to travel a good deal, with a few nights spent on the road or even a few weeks spent out of the country. Technicians at banks or data-processing services usually work in clean, pleasant surroundings. The technician who goes into farm management or who owns a farm is likely to work outdoors in all kinds of weather.

Agribusiness technicians are often confronted with problems requiring careful thought and decision. They must be able to remain calm when things get hectic, to make sound decisions, and then to stand by their decisions in the face of possible disagreement. It is a profession that requires initiative, self-reliance, and the ability to accept responsibilities that may bring blame at times of failure as well as substantial rewards for successful performance. For those technicians who possess the qualities of leadership and a strong interest in the agricultural business, it can be a challenging, exciting, and highly satisfying profession.

OUTLOOK

According to the DOL, agribusiness provides employment to about 21 percent of the country's labor force. Despite the fluctuations in the agricultural industry, agribusiness professionals and technicians will continue to be in demand in the marketing and production of food and other agricultural products.

Agribusiness technicians may find more opportunities to work abroad; agribusiness plays a large part in global trade issues and in the government's efforts to support farms and agricultural reforms in other countries. Agribusiness construction is a subfield that is developing as a result of these reforms; technicians will be needed to assist in the planning and construction of farm-to-market roads in other countries, irrigation channels, bridges, grain silos, and other improvements.

FOR MORE INFORMATION

To learn about the roles economists play in agriculture, visit the AAEA Web site.
Agricultural and Applied Economics Association (AAEA)
555 East Wells Street, Suite 1100
Milwaukee, WI 53202
Tel: 414-918-3190
E-mail: info@aaea.org
http://www.aaea.org

For more information on opportunities in the agricultural field and education, contact
4-H
U.S. Department of Agriculture
National Institute of Food and Agriculture
1400 Independence Avenue, SW, Stop 2225
Washington, DC 20250-2225
Tel: 202-401-4114
E-mail: 4hhq@nifa.usda.gov
http://www.national4-hheadquarters.gov and http://4-h.org

For information on careers and chapter membership, contact
National FFA Organization
6060 FFA Drive
PO Box 68960
Indianapolis, IN 46268-0960

Tel: 317-802-6060
https://www.ffa.org

For information on the agricultural industry, contact
U.S. Department of Agriculture
1400 Independence Avenue, SW
Washington, DC 20250-0002
Tel: 202-720-2791
http://www.usda.gov

Agricultural Economists

QUICK FACTS

School Subjects
Agriculture
Business
Economics
Mathematics

Personal Skills
Communication/ideas
Technical/scientific

Work Environment
Indoors and outdoors
One location with some
travel

Minimum Education Level
Master's degree

Salary Range
$42,820 to $86,930 to
$153,210+

Certification or Licensing
None available

Outlook
More slowly than the average

DOT
050

GOE
02.04.02

NOC
4162

O*NET-SOC
19-3011.00, 25-1063.00

OVERVIEW

Economists are concerned with how society uses resources such as land, labor, raw materials, and machinery to produce goods and services for consumption and production in the present and future. Economists study how economic systems address three basic questions: "What shall we produce?" "How shall we produce it?" and "For whom shall we produce it?" The economist then compiles, processes, and interprets the answers to these questions. *Agricultural economists* are specialized economists who study food production, development in rural areas, and the allocation of natural resources. They conduct research and surveys as well as create economic models to make short- and long-term forecasts for the agricultural economy. Some agricultural economists contribute to trade journals and newspapers, teach at the college level, or conduct research. There are about 14,600 economists employed in the United States. Agricultural economists make up only a small percentage of this total.

HISTORY

Economics deals with the struggle to divide up a finite amount of goods and services to satisfy an unlimited amount of human needs and desires. No society, no matter how rich and successful, is able to produce everything needed or wanted by individuals. This reality was evident to people throughout history. In ancient Greece, the philosopher Plato dis-

14

cussed economic topics in his work, *The Republic*, saying the division of labor among people was the only way to supply a larger need. Individuals, he said, are not naturally self-sufficient and thus they need to cooperate in their efforts and exchange goods and services.

It was not until 1776 that the theory of economics was given a name. Adam Smith, in his work *Wealth of Nations*, described that individuals, given the opportunity to trade freely, will not create chaos. Instead, he claimed that free trade results in an orderly, logical system. His belief in this free trade system has been interpreted as an endorsement of laissez-faire capitalism, which discourages government restrictions on trade. Other economists believe that regulation is necessary to limit corruption and unfair or monopolistic practices.

The importance of economics is evidenced by its status as the only social science in which a Nobel Prize is awarded. In the last century, economics has come to be used in making a broad array of decisions within businesses, government agencies, and many other kinds of organizations.

Agricultural economics emerged as a subdiscipline of economics in the late 1800s as government officials and agricultural professionals sought to improve crop production. Henry Charles Taylor is considered the "father of agricultural economics" in the United States. He established the first postsecondary agricultural economics program in the United States at the University of Wisconsin–Madison in 1909. (See Profile: Henry Charles Taylor for more information.) The Agricultural & Applied Economics Association was founded in 1910 to represent the professional interests of agricultural economists.

THE JOB

The cultivation and harvesting of crops is a necessity since we all need food in order to live. However, agriculture is also an important business. It's no wonder then that government agencies, agricultural producers, and the general public rely on agricultural economists to provide them with information regarding the supply and demand for agricultural goods and services and how they are produced, distributed, and consumed in the United States and throughout the world.

Agricultural economists working for the U.S. Department of Agriculture (USDA) create forecasts regarding the supply and demand of certain goods. They analyze the economic implications of agricultural policies and advise agricultural organizations and companies, government agencies, and food producers about available options regarding production costs and cultivation options.

Profile: Henry Charles Taylor (1873–1969)

Henry Charles Taylor is considered by many to be the "father of agricultural economics." He grew up in rural Iowa, the son of a well-to-do farmer.

After studying agriculture and economics in college, Taylor traveled throughout Europe, touring area farms by bicycle. Around this time he wrote his first doctoral dissertation, "The Decline of Land Owner Farmers in England."

Taylor was instrumental in creating the first college agricultural economics department in the United States at the University of Wisconsin–Madison in 1909. Taylor also authored the first agricultural economics textbook.

In 1919, Taylor took a position with the USDA. Some of his achievements included the expansion of agricultural information services, the improvement of data management of world agricultural production and consumption, and the standardization of crop grading.

After he left the USDA, Taylor served in leadership positions in several agricultural-related organizations, including the Farm Foundation and the American Country Life Association.

Source: U.S. Department of Agriculture

Agricultural economists may be assigned to study a variety of crops or a single crop—rice, for example. Rice is the primary food staple for half the world's population. While people in practically every country consume rice, each culture has its own preference for a particular variety or varieties. In the United States, rice is grown in four regions, with each region specializing in a specific type—either long-, medium-, or short-grain. Agricultural economists are interested in such information, including the way rice crops are planted, harvested, and processed prior to export or domestic use.

The methods agricultural economists use to obtain information vary according to the goal of the project or study. Regarding rice crops, agricultural economists may travel to different U.S. regions to learn how farmers grow rice. Questions asked by agricultural economists include the following: What types of rice are grown? What type of soil and irrigation methods are used to grow the rice? Are fertilizers or pesticides used? If so, what products and what amounts are applied to farmland? What are the planting and harvesting cycles for the rice crop?

Agricultural economists gather data, sometimes consulting with farmers, mill operators and other processing agents, and food scientists. Agricultural economists use various sampling techniques to conduct surveys on individual rice preferences, such as the length of grain or its taste or fragrance. They also use existing data and research on rice production to prepare reports regarding rice sales in the United States and abroad.

Agricultural economists interpret research data, study agricultural samples, and create economic models using computer software in order to develop short- and long-term forecasts. Farmers use these forecasts when deciding on new crop varieties to cultivate; mill owners use them when setting prices for the coming year. Agricultural economists also track the costs related to the cultivation of a particular crop—such as labor, fuel, fertilizer, and seed—which affect profit margins for farmers.

Agricultural economists also consider public tastes and preferences when conducting research. In the case of rice, while most rice grown in the United States is the short-grain variety, long-grained jasmine or basmati rice is imported from other countries—mainly Thailand and India. Agricultural economists track import statistics to predict future demand for these varieties. Further research and samplings might find other reasons for this growing demand, such as the increase of immigrants to the United States who prefer this type of rice or a growing interest in Indian- or Thai-influenced cooking on television cooking shows or in food magazines. Agricultural economists use these statistics to encourage rice farmers to consider growing long-grain rice in addition to their current short-grain crops. The statistics may also be of interest to U.S. rice breeders, who might be encouraged to develop new varieties easily grown in the United States that have characteristics similar to Asian varieties.

Agricultural economists also monitor the growth and profits of rice growers in other countries. They track the quality and quantity of foreign crops as compared to those in the United States. How each rice crop compares, country to country, is important to agricultural economists since it is an indication to how the United States can complete in the global market.

Agricultural economists use computers to create charts and graphs, maintain databases, and complete modeling systems. In addition, they create written reports that summarize their findings and forecasts. Some agricultural economists write for industry journals and newspapers. Many times, mainstream journalists contact them to gain information on agricultural market trends. Some choose to teach at the university level, or present their research at

An agricultural economist uses computer software to study crop-planting systems. *(Peggy Greb, USDA, Agricultural Research Service)*

conferences and industry seminars. Others work as retail managers, sales representatives, and financial lenders, planners, and analysts for agriculture-related organizations and companies.

REQUIREMENTS

High School
A strong college preparatory program is necessary in high school if you wish to enter this field. Courses in other social sciences, economics, statistics, accounting, mathematics, and English are extremely important to a would-be economist, since analyzing, interpreting, and expressing one's informed opinions about many different kinds of data are primary tasks for someone employed in this field. Students who want to specialize in agricultural economics should take classes in agriculture, biology, economics, and earth science. Also, take computer science classes so that you will be able to use this research tool in college and later on. Finally, since you will be heading off to college and probably postgraduate studies, consider taking a foreign language to round out your educational background.

Postsecondary Training
A bachelor's degree with a major in economics is the minimum requirement for an entry-level position such as research assistant.

A master's degree, or even a Ph.D., is more commonly required for most positions as an economist.

Typically, an economics major takes at least 10 courses on various economic topics, plus two or more mathematics courses, such as statistics and calculus or algebra. The federal government requires candidates for entry-level economist positions to have a minimum of 21 semester hours of economics and three hours of statistics, accounting, or calculus. Graduate-level courses include such specialties as advanced economic theory, econometrics, international economics, and labor economics.

Those who are interested in becoming agricultural economists typically earn a bachelor's degree in economics, environmental economics and policy, resource economics, business, or a related field and then pursue a graduate-level degree in agricultural economics. Visit http://www.aaea.org/outreach/programs.php for a list of colleges and universities in the United States and Canada that offer programs in agricultural and applied economics.

Other Requirements

Agricultural economists' work is detail oriented. They do extensive research and enjoy working with abstract theories. Their research work must be precise and well documented. In addition, economists must be able to clearly explain their ideas to a range of people, including other economic experts, political leaders, and even students in a classroom.

EXPLORING

You can augment your interest in economics by taking related courses in social science and mathematics and by becoming informed about business, economic, and agricultural industry trends through reading business-related publications such as newspaper business sections and business magazines and publications that focus on agriculture. Some specialized publications that focus on agricultural economics include *American Journal of Agricultural Economics, Applied Economic Perspectives and Policy,* and *Choices,* which are published by the Agricultural & Applied Economics Association. Visit http://www.aaea.org/publications for more information. In addition to economics course work, college students can participate in specific programs and extracurricular activities sponsored by their university's business school, such as internships with government agencies (including the USDA) and agriculture-related clubs and organizations.

EMPLOYERS

Approximately 14,600 economists are employed in the United States. Agricultural economists make up only a small percentage of this total. Typical employers of agricultural economists include government agencies (such as for the USDA's Economic Research Service), financial institutions, food and agribusiness firms, food retailers and manufacturers, and agribusiness firms. Many agricultural economists teach at colleges and universities. Others work for international organizations, such as the United Nations and the U.S. Agency for International Development.

STARTING OUT

The journals and Web sites of the various professional economic associations (including the Agricultural & Applied Economics Association) are good sources of job opportunities for beginning economists. Your school's career services office can also assist you in locating internships and in setting up interviews with potential employers.

ADVANCEMENT

An agricultural economist's advancement depends on his or her training, experience, personal interests, and ambition. All specialized areas provide opportunities for promotion to jobs requiring more skill and competence. Such jobs are characterized by more administrative, research, or advisory responsibilities. Consequently, promotions are governed to a great extent by job performance in the beginning fields of work. In university-level academic positions, publishing papers and books about one's research is necessary to become tenured.

EARNINGS

Economists are among the highest paid social scientists. According to the U.S. Department of Labor (DOL), the median salary for economists was $86,930 in 2009. The lowest paid 10 percent made less than $44,720, and the highest paid 10 percent earned more than $153,210. The DOL reports that economists employed by the federal government earned mean annual salaries of $106,170. College economics educators earned salaries that ranged from less than $42,820 to $144,750 or more. Benefits such as vacation and health insurance are comparable to those of workers in other organizations.

WORK ENVIRONMENT

Agricultural economists conduct much of their work indoors, collecting research and statistics, creating charts and reports, and updating computer databases. They often field phone calls from journalists seeking data, or answer queries from government officials. Travel, sometimes to foreign countries, is necessary, especially when the project at hand requires field research or meetings with government officials or scientists. The work can be stressful with long hours, especially when economists are faced with project deadlines. Agricultural economists also travel to attend industry seminars or conferences.

Agricultural economists often consult and collaborate with other economists, government officials, food and agricultural scientists, and farmers. They are often assigned assistants to help them in their work.

OUTLOOK

The employment of economists is expected to grow more slowly than average for all occupations through 2018, according to the DOL. Most openings will occur as economists retire, transfer to other job fields, or leave the profession for other reasons. Economists employed by private industry—especially in management, scientific, and technical consulting services—will enjoy the best prospects. In the academic arena, economists with master's and doctoral degrees will face strong competition for desirable teaching jobs. The demand for secondary school economics teachers is expected to grow. Economics majors with only bachelor's degrees will experience the greatest employment difficulty, although their analytical skills can lead to positions in related fields such as management and sales. Those who meet state certification requirements may wish to become secondary school economics teachers, as demand for teachers in this specialty is expected to increase.

FOR MORE INFORMATION

For information on careers and a list of colleges that offer programs in the field, contact
American Agricultural Economics Association
555 East Wells Street, Suite 1100
Milwaukee, WI 53202-3800
Tel: 414-918-3190

E-mail: info@aaea.org
http://www.aaea.org

For information on job listings and resources of interest to economists, contact
American Economic Association
2014 Broadway, Suite 305
Nashville, TN 37203-2425
Tel: 615-322-2595
E-mail: aeainfo@vanderbilt.edu
http://www.aeaweb.org

For information on graduate programs in environmental and resource economics, contact
Association of Environmental and Resource Economists
1616 P Street, NW, Room 600
Washington, DC 20036-1434
Tel: 202-328-5125
http://www.aere.org

The council promotes the economic education of students from kindergarten through 12th grade. It offers teacher training courses and materials. For more information, contact
Council for Economic Education
122 East 42 Street, Suite 2600
New York, NY 10168-2699
Tel: 800-338-1192
http://www.councilforeconed.org

To read the publication Careers in Business Economics, *contact or check out the following Web site:*
National Association for Business Economics
1233 20th Street, NW, Suite 505
Washington, DC 20036-2365
Tel: 202-463-6223
E-mail: nabe@nabe.com
http://www.nabe.com

For information on membership and job listings, contact
Society of Government Economists
PO Box 77082
Washington, DC 20013-8082

Tel: 202-643-1743
http://www.sge-econ.org

For information on the agricultural industry, contact
U.S. Department of Agriculture
1400 Independence Avenue, SW
Washington, DC 20250-0002
Tel: 202-720-2791
http://www.usda.gov

For information on career opportunities in Canada, contact
Canadian Agricultural Economics Society
Department of Economics
University of Victoria
Room 360, Business and Economics Building
PO Box 1700, STN CSC
Victoria, BC V8W 2Y2 Canada
http://caes.usask.ca

Agricultural Equipment Technicians

QUICK FACTS

School Subjects
Mathematics
Technical/shop

Personal Skills
Mechanical/manipulative
Technical/scientific

Work Environment
Indoors and outdoors
Primarily multiple locations

Minimum Education Level
Some postsecondary training

Salary Range
$21,880 to $32,970 to
$48,070+

Certification or Licensing
None available

Outlook
About as fast as the average

DOT
624

GOE
03.03.01, 05.03.01

NOC
7316

O*NET-SOC
45-2091.00, 49-3041.00

OVERVIEW

Agricultural equipment technicians work with modern farm machinery. They assemble, adjust, operate, maintain, modify, test, and even help design it. This machinery includes automatic animal feeding systems; milking machine systems; and tilling, planting, harvesting, irrigating, drying, and handling equipment. Agricultural equipment technicians work on farms or for agricultural machinery manufacturers or dealerships. They often supervise skilled mechanics and other workers who keep machines and systems operating at maximum efficiency.

HISTORY

The history of farming equipment stretches back to prehistoric times, when the first agricultural workers developed the sickle. In the Middle Ages, the horse-drawn plow greatly increased farm production, and in the early 1700s, Jethro Tull designed and built the first mechanical seed planter, further increasing production. The Industrial Revolution brought advances in the design and use of specialized machinery for strenuous and repetitive work. It had a great impact on the agricultural industry, beginning in 1831 with Cyrus McCormick's invention of the reaper.

In the first half of the 20th century, governmental experiment stations developed high-yield, standardized varieties of farm crops. This, combined with the establishment of agricultural equipment-producing companies, caused a boom in the production of farm

24

machinery. In the late 1930s, the abundance of inexpensive petro-
leum spurred the development of gasoline- and diesel-run farm
machinery. During the early 1940s, the resulting explosion in
complex and powerful farm machinery multiplied production and
replaced most of the horses and mules used on farms in the United
States.

Modern farming is heavily dependent on very complex and expensive machinery. Highly trained and skilled technicians and farm
mechanics are therefore required to install, operate, maintain, and
modify this machinery, thereby ensuring the nation's farm productivity. Recent developments in agricultural mechanization and automation make the career of agricultural equipment technicians both
challenging and rewarding. Sophisticated machines are being used
to plant, cultivate, harvest, and process food; to contour, drain, and
renovate land; and to clear land and harvest forest products in the
process. Qualified agricultural equipment technicians are needed
not only to service and sell this equipment, but also to manage it on
the farm.

Farming has increasingly become a highly competitive, big business. A successful farmer may have hundreds of thousands or even
millions of dollars invested in land and machinery. For this investment to pay off, it is vital to keep the machinery in excellent operating condition. Prompt and reliable service from the farm equipment
manufacturer and dealer is necessary for the success of both farmer
and dealer. Interruptions or delays because of poor service are costly
for everyone involved. To provide good service, manufacturers and
dealers need technicians and specialists who possess agricultural and
engineering knowledge in addition to technical skills.

THE JOB

Agricultural equipment technicians work in a wide variety of jobs
both on and off the farm. In general, most agricultural equipment
technicians find employment in one of three areas: equipment manufacturing, equipment sales and service, and on-farm equipment
management.

Equipment manufacturing technicians are involved primarily
with the design and testing of agricultural equipment such as farm
machinery; irrigation, power, and electrification systems; soil and
water conservation equipment; and agricultural harvesting and
processing equipment. There are two kinds of technicians working
in this field: agricultural engineering technicians and agricultural
equipment test technicians.

Common Farm Equipment
Some of the machinery used on farms is as follows:

- Balers: Used for cutting and baling hay, straw, and silage
- Forage harvesters: Used for cutting and harvesting corn and hay
- Disk harrows: After plowing, smoothes out and levels a field for planting
- Chisel plows: Used for field tillage
- Field cultivators: Prepares the soil for seeding

Agricultural engineering technicians work under the supervision of design engineers. They prepare original layouts and complete detailed drawings of agricultural equipment. They also review plans, diagrams, and blueprints to ensure that new products comply with company standards and design specifications. In order to do this, they must use their knowledge of biological, engineering, and design principles. They also must keep current on all of the new equipment and materials being developed for the industry to make sure the machines run at their highest capacity.

Agricultural equipment test technicians test and evaluate the performance of agricultural machinery and equipment. In particular, they make sure the equipment conforms with operating requirements, such as horsepower, resistance to vibration, and strength and hardness of parts. They test equipment under actual field conditions on company-operated research farms and under more controlled conditions. They work with test equipment and recording instruments such as bend-fatigue machines, dynamometers, strength testers, hardness meters, analytical balances, and electronic recorders.

Test technicians are also trained in methods of recording the data gathered during these tests. They compute values such as horsepower and tensile strength using algebraic formulas and report their findings using graphs, tables, and sketches.

After the design and testing phases are complete, other agricultural equipment technicians work with engineers to perform any necessary adjustments in the equipment design. By performing these functions under the general supervision of the design engineer, technicians do the engineers' "detective work" so the engineers can devote more time to research and development.

Large agricultural machinery companies may employ agricultural equipment technicians to supervise production, assembly, and plant operations.

Most manufacturers market their products through regional sales organizations to individual dealers. Technicians may serve as *sales representatives* of regional sales offices, where they are assigned a number of dealers in a given territory and sell agricultural equipment directly to them. They may also conduct sales-training programs for the dealers to help them become more effective salespeople.

These technicians are also qualified to work in sales positions within dealerships, either as *equipment sales workers* or *parts clerks*. They are required to perform equipment demonstrations for customers. They also appraise the value of used equipment for trade-in allowances. Technicians in these positions may advance to sales or parts manager positions.

Some technicians involved in sales become *systems specialists*, who work for equipment dealerships, assisting farmers in the planning and installation of various kinds of mechanized systems, such as irrigation or materials-handling systems, grain bins, or drying systems.

In the service area, technicians may work as *field service representatives*, forming a liaison between the companies they represent and the dealers. They assist the dealers in product warranty work, diagnose service problems, and give seminars or workshops on new service information and techniques. These types of service technicians may begin their careers as specialists in certain kinds of repairs. *Hydraulic specialists*, for instance, maintain and repair the component parts of hydraulic systems in tractors and other agricultural machines. *Diesel specialists* rebuild, calibrate, and test diesel pumps, injectors, and other diesel engine components.

Many service technicians work as service managers or parts department managers. *Service managers* assign duties to the repair workers, diagnose machinery problems, estimate repair costs for customers, and manage the repair shop.

Parts department managers in equipment dealerships maintain inventories of all the parts that may be requested either by customers or by the service departments of the dealership. They deal directly with customers, parts suppliers, and dealership managers and must have good sales and purchasing skills. They also must be effective business managers.

Technicians working on the farm have various responsibilities, the most important of which is keeping machinery in top working condition during the growing season. During off-season periods they may overhaul or modify equipment or simply keep the machinery in good working order for the next season.

Some technicians find employment as *on-farm machinery managers*, usually working on large farms servicing or supervising the servicing of all automated equipment. They also monitor the field operation of all machines and keep complete records of costs, utilization, and repair procedures relating to the maintenance of each piece of mechanical equipment.

REQUIREMENTS

High School
You should take as many mathematics, technical/shop, and mechanical drawing classes as you can. Take science classes, including courses in earth science, to gain some insight into agriculture, soil conservation, and the environment. Look into adult education programs available to high school students; in such a program, you may be able to enroll in preengineering courses.

Postsecondary Training
A high school diploma is necessary, and some college and specialized experience is also important. A four-year education, along with some continuing education courses, can be very helpful in pursuing work, particularly if you're seeking jobs with the government.

Postsecondary education for the agricultural equipment technician should include courses in general agriculture, agricultural power and equipment, practical engineering, hydraulics, agricultural-equipment business methods, electrical equipment, engineering, social science, economics, and sales techniques. On-the-job experience during the summer is invaluable and frequently is included as part of the regular curriculum in these programs. Students are placed on farms, functioning as technicians-in-training. They also may work in farm equipment dealerships where their time is divided between the sales, parts, and service departments. Occupational experience, one of the most important phases of the postsecondary training program, gives students an opportunity to discover which field best suits them and which phase of the business they prefer. Upon completion of this program, most technical and community colleges award an associate's degree.

Other Requirements
The work of the agricultural equipment technician is similar to that of an engineer. You must have knowledge of physical science and

engineering principles and enough mathematical background to work with these principles. You must have a working knowledge of farm crops, machinery, and all agricultural-related products. You should be detail oriented. You should also have people skills, as you'll be working closely with professionals, other technicians, and farmers.

EXPLORING

If you live in a farming community, you've probably already had some experience with farming equipment. Vocational agriculture education programs in high schools can be found in most rural settings, many suburban settings, and even in some urban schools. The teaching staff and counselors in these schools can provide considerable information about this career.

Light industrial machinery is now used in almost every industry. It is always helpful to watch machinery being used and to talk with people who own, operate, and repair it.

Summer and part-time work on a farm, in an agricultural equipment manufacturing plant, or in an equipment sales and service business offers opportunities to work on or near agricultural and light industrial machinery. Such a job may provide you with a clearer idea about the various activities, challenges, rewards, and possible limitations of this career.

EMPLOYERS

Depending on their area of specialization, technicians work for engineers, manufacturers, scientists, sales and services companies, and farmers. They can also find work with government agencies, such as the U.S. Department of Agriculture.

STARTING OUT

It is still possible to enter this career by starting as an inexperienced worker in a machinery manufacturer's plant or on a farm and learning machine technician skills on the job. However, this approach is becoming increasingly difficult due to the complexity of modern machinery. Because of this, some formal classroom training is usually necessary, and many people find it difficult to complete even part-time study of the field's theory and science while also working a full-time job.

Operators and managers of large, well-equipped farms and farm equipment companies in need of employees keep in touch with colleges offering agricultural equipment programs. Students who do well during their occupational experience period usually have an excellent chance of going to work for the same employer after graduation. Many colleges have an interview day on which personnel representatives of manufacturers, distributors, farm owners or managers, and dealers are invited to recruit students completing technician programs. In general, any student who does well in a training program can expect employment immediately upon graduation.

ADVANCEMENT

Opportunities for advancement and self-employment are excellent for those with the initiative to keep abreast of continuing developments in the farm equipment field. Technicians often attend company schools in sales and service or take advanced evening courses in colleges.

EARNINGS

Agricultural technicians working for the government may be able to enter a position at the GS-5 (government wage scale) level, which was $27,431 in 2010. The U.S. Department of Labor reports that median annual earnings for agricultural equipment mechanics were $32,970 in 2009. Hourly wages ranged from less than $10.52 ($21,880 a year) to more than $23.11 ($48,070 a year). Those working on farms often receive room and board as a supplement to their annual salary. The salary that technicians eventually receive depends—as do most salaries—on individual ability, initiative, and the supply of skilled technicians in the field of work or locality. There is opportunity to work overtime during planting and harvesting seasons.

In addition to their salaries, most technicians receive fringe benefits such as health and retirement packages, paid vacations, and other benefits similar to those received by engineering technicians. Technicians employed in sales are usually paid a commission in addition to their base salary.

WORK ENVIRONMENT

Working conditions vary according to the type of field chosen. Technicians who are employed by large farming operations will work indoors or outdoors depending on the season and the tasks that need to be done. Planning machine overhauls and the directing of such work usually are done in enclosed spaces equipped for it. As implied by its name, field servicing and repairs are done in the field.

Some agricultural equipment sales representatives work in their own or nearby communities, while others must travel extensively.

Technicians in agricultural equipment research, development, and production usually work under typical factory conditions: some work in an office or laboratory; others work in a manufacturing plant; or, in some cases, field testing and demonstration are performed where the machinery will be used.

For technicians who assemble, adjust, modify, or test equipment and for those who provide customer service, application studies, and maintenance services, the surroundings may be similar to large automobile service centers.

In all cases, safety precautions must be a constant concern. Appropriate clothing, an acute awareness of one's environment, and careful lifting or hoisting of heavy machinery must be standard. While safety practices have improved greatly over the years, certain risks do exist. Heavy lifting may cause injury, and burns and cuts are always possible. The surroundings may be noisy and grimy. Some work is performed in cramped or awkward physical positions. Gasoline fumes and odors from oil products are a constant factor. Most technicians ordinarily work a 40-hour week, but emergency repairs may require overtime.

OUTLOOK

Employment of agricultural equipment technicians is expected to grow about as fast as the average for all careers through 2018, according to the *Occupational Outlook Handbook*. Today, agricultural equipment businesses demand more expertise than ever before. A variety of complex specialized machines and mechanical devices are steadily being produced and modified to help farmers improve the quality and productivity of their labor. These machines require trained technicians to design, produce, test, sell, and service them. Trained workers also are needed to instruct the final owners in their proper repair, operation, and maintenance.

In addition, the agricultural industry is adopting advanced computer, hydraulics, and electronic technology. Computer skills are becoming more and more useful in this field. Precision farming will also require specialized training as more agricultural equipment becomes linked to satellite systems.

As agriculture becomes more technical, the agricultural equipment technician will assume an increasingly vital role in helping farmers solve problems that interfere with efficient production. These opportunities exist not only in the United States, but also worldwide. As agricultural economies everywhere become mechanized, inventive technicians with training in modern business principles will find expanding employment opportunities abroad.

FOR MORE INFORMATION

To read equipment sales statistics, agricultural reports, and other news of interest to agricultural equipment technicians, visit
Association of Equipment Manufacturers
6737 West Washington Street, Suite 2400
Milwaukee, WI 53214-5647
Tel: 414-272-0943
E-mail: aem@aem.org
http://www.aem.org

Visit the following Web site to learn about publications and read industry news:
Farm Equipment Manufacturers Association
1000 Executive Parkway, Suite 100
St. Louis, MO 63141-6369
Tel: 314-878-2304
E-mail: info@farmequip.org
http://www.farmequip.org

For information on student chapters and the many activities it offers, contact
National FFA Organization
6060 FFA Drive
PO Box 68960
Indianapolis, IN 46268-0960
Tel: 317-802-6060
E-mail: membership@ffa.org
https://www.ffa.org

For information on the agricultural industry, contact
U.S. Department of Agriculture
1400 Independence Avenue, SW
Washington, DC 20250-0002
Tel: 202-720-2791
http://www.usda.gov

Agricultural Pilots

OVERVIEW

Agricultural pilots, also called *ag pilots, crop dusters,* and *aerial applicators,* perform flying jobs related to the farming industry. They are skilled professionals who operate aircraft for such purposes as transporting cargo to market, aerial applications, hauling feed, or planting seed. In addition to flying aircraft, agricultural pilots perform a variety of safety-related tasks involving both the aircraft and the cargo. They may be self-employed or work for large pest control companies or government agencies. There are approximately 3,000 agricultural pilots employed in the United States.

HISTORY

The history of agricultural aviation is, naturally, tied to that of modern aviation. This period is generally considered to have begun with the flight of Orville and Wilbur Wright's heavier-than-air machine on December 17, 1903. On that day, the Wright brothers flew their machine four times and became the first airplane pilots. In the early days of aviation, the pilot's job was quite different from that of the pilot of today. As he flew the plane, for example, Orville Wright was lying on his stomach in the middle of the bottom wing of the plane. There was a strap across his hips, and to turn the plane, he had to tilt his hips from side to side—hardly the way today's pilot makes a turn.

The aviation industry developed rapidly as designers raced to improve upon the Wright brothers' design. During the early years of flight, many aviators earned a living as "barnstormers," entertaining people with stunts and taking passengers on short flights around the countryside. As airplanes became more dependable, they were adapted for a variety of purposes such as use in the military and for the U.S. government-run airmail service. According to the National Agricultural Aviation Association, the first time a plane was used to spread pesticide was in 1921. In an experiment conducted by the military, lead arsenate dust was spread by plane to stop a moth infestation in Ohio. By 1923 crop dusting was being done on a commercial basis.

Today planes used for agricultural aviation are specifically designed for that purpose. They can carry hundreds of gallons of pesticides and are equipped with the latest technology, such as the global positioning system (GPS). Unlike the crop-dusting process of the past, which used dry chemicals, today's process typically involves liquid pesticides and other controlling products as well as nutrition sprays. Advances in agricultural aviation have allowed U.S. farms to become increasingly productive.

THE JOB

Agricultural pilots perform a number of duties that benefit the farming industry. They help farmers prevent crop damage. Some work for pest control companies while others are self-employed. In farm work, agricultural pilots spray chemicals over crops and orchards to fertilize them, control plant diseases or weeds, and control pests. They also drop seeds into fields to plant crops.

It's a Bug's Life

Though many bugs are harmful to plants, some can be beneficial. These bugs prey on plant-feeding insects, which, as you'll read, usually isn't pretty.

- Ladybugs: Eat aphids, mealy bugs, and mites; adult ladybugs may eat 50 or more aphids a day
- Praying mantis: Kill their plant-feeding prey by biting the back of the neck, severing the main nerves
- Lacewings: Suck the body fluids from their prey and carry the remains of their victims on their backs
- Hover flies: Grasp plant-feeding insects and puncture them with tiny hooks in their mouths

A crop duster sprays a field of crops. *(Dave Martin, AP Photo)*

Before agricultural pilots begin the process of spraying farmland, they must survey the area for buildings, hills, power lines, and other obstacles and hazards. They must also notify residents and businesses in the general area that they will spray so that people and animals can be moved away from target areas.

Some agricultural pilots, particularly those who work for pest control companies, may mix their own chemicals, using their knowledge of what mixture may be best for certain types of plants, plant or soil conditions, or pest problems.

Agricultural pilots fly helicopters and small, turboprop planes, which are slower compared to larger, transport craft, but which are good for flying close to the ground and for carrying heavy loads. They must fly close to the ground, often only a few feet above a crop, so that they will only hit designated areas with the chemicals.

Agricultural pilots help farmers by dropping food over pastures. They may photograph wildlife or count game animals for conservation programs. And their work also extends into forests, fields, and swamps, where herbicides and insecticides are needed. They also fight forest fires by dumping water or fire-retardant materials over burning areas.

No matter what the job, pilots must determine weather and flight conditions, make sure that sufficient fuel is on board to complete the flight safely, and verify the maintenance status of the airplane before each flight. They perform system checks to test the proper functioning of instrumentation and electronic and mechanical systems on the plane.

Once all of these preflight duties are done, the pilot taxis the aircraft to the designated runway and prepares for takeoff. Takeoff speeds must be calculated based on the aircraft's weight, which is affected by the weight of the cargo being carried.

During flights, agricultural pilots must constantly be aware of their surroundings since they fly so close to the ground and frequently are near hazards such as power lines. They need good judgment to deal with any emergency situations that might arise. They monitor aircraft systems, keep an eye on the weather conditions, and perform the job of the flight, such as spraying fertilizer.

Once the pilot has landed and taxied to the appropriate area, he or she follows a "shutdown" checklist of procedures. Pilots also keep logs of their flight hours. Those who are self-employed or work for smaller companies are typically responsible for refueling the airplane, performing maintenance, and keeping business records.

REQUIREMENTS

High School

There are a number of classes you can take in high school to help prepare you for becoming a pilot. You should take science classes, such as chemistry and physics, as well as mathematics, such as algebra and geometry. Take computer classes to familiarize yourself with various programs. Since you will be responsible for the maintenance and care of a plane, you may also benefit from taking an electronics shop class or other shop class where you get to work on engines. Take English classes to improve your research and writing skills. Throughout your career you will need to study flying or repair manuals, file reports, and communicate with customers. Since you may be responsible for record keeping, take business or accounting classes. If your school offers agriculture classes, take any that will teach you about soils, crops, and growing methods.

Postsecondary Training

Many companies that employ pilots prefer to hire candidates with at least two years of college training. Courses in engineering, meteorology, physics, mathematics, and agriculture are helpful in preparing for this career. In addition to these courses, you will need training as a pilot. There are approximately 600 civilian flying schools certified by the Federal Aviation Administration (FAA), including some colleges and universities that offer degree credit for pilot training. A number of schools offer training specifically in agricultural aviation. Some people take up this career after leaving the military, where they trained as pilots.

The National Agricultural Aviation Association offers information on training requirements and schools at its Web site, http://www.agaviation.org.

Certification or Licensing

Agricultural pilots must hold a commercial pilot's license from the FAA. A fairly long and rigorous process is involved in obtaining a commercial license. The first step in this process is to receive flying instruction.

If you are 16 or over and can pass the rigid mandatory physical examination, you may apply for permission to take flying instruction. This instruction consists of classroom education and flight training from a FAA-certified flight instructor.

Before you make your first solo flight, you must get a medical certificate (certifying that you are in good health) and an instructor-endorsed student pilot certificate. In order to get the student pilot certificate, you must pass a test given by the flight instructor. This test will have questions about FAA rules as well as questions about the model and make of the aircraft you will fly. If you pass the test and the instructor feels you are prepared to make a solo flight, the instructor will endorse your pilot certificate and logbook.

To apply for a private pilot's license, you must take a written examination. To qualify for it, you must be at least 17 years of age, successfully fulfill a solo flying requirement of 20 hours or more, and meet instrument flying and cross-country flying requirements.

The next step in getting a commercial license is to continue to log flying time and increase your knowledge and skills. To receive your commercial license you must be at least 18 years of age, have 250 hours of flying time, and successfully complete a number of exams. These tests include a physical exam; a written test given by the FAA covering such topics as safe flight operations, navigation principles, and federal aviation regulations; and a practical test to demonstrate your flying skills. Pilots must also receive a rating for the kind of plane they can fly (such as single-engine or multiengine). In addition, a commercial pilot needs an instrument rating by the FAA and a restricted radio telephone operator's permit by the Federal Communications Commission (FCC). In states where they spray restricted pesticides, agricultural pilots must be certified by the U.S. Department of Agriculture.

Other Requirements

All pilots must be of sound physical and emotional health. They need excellent eyesight and eye-hand coordination as well as excellent hearing and normal heart rate and blood pressure. The successful agricultural pilot is also detail oriented since much paperwork, planning, and following of regulations is involved in this job. Those who are self-employed or working for smaller companies may find that they have frequent contact with customers, and so they must be able to work well with others. Naturally, an agricultural pilot should have an interest in farming methods and the environment as well as a love of flying. Good judgment is essential for this work.

EXPLORING

You can explore this field through a number of activities. Join groups such as your high school aviation club and the National FFA Organization (formerly Future Farmers of America). These groups may give you the opportunity to meet with professionals in the field, learn about farm products and management, and find others with similar interests. Read publications related to these industries such as the magazines *Agricultural Aviation* (http://www.agaviation. org/content/news-publications), *AgAir Update* (http://www.agairup date.com), and *The Progressive Farmer* (http://www.dtnprogressive farmer.com/dtnag). If you have the financial resources, you can take flying lessons once you are 16 and have passed a physical exam. Also, consider learning how to operate a ham radio. This skill will help you when you apply for your restricted radio operator's permit, a requirement for commercial pilots.

EMPLOYERS

Approximately 3,000 agricultural pilots are employed in the United States. California and the southern states, where the crop-growing season lasts longest, are where agricultural pilots find the most work. They also find some work with northern crops and in forests of the northeastern and western states. Many are employed by crop-dusting companies; others are self-employed. Federal and state government departments also employ agricultural pilots to assist with environmental, conservation, and preservation needs.

STARTING OUT

It is not unusual for people to enter this field after gaining experience in the agricultural industry itself, working on farms and learning about crop production while they also develop their flying skills. Others enter with flying as their first love and are drawn to the challenge of agricultural aviation. Once pilots have completed their training, they may find that contacts made through aviation schools lead to job openings. Those who have the financial means can begin by opening their own business. Equipment, however, is very expensive—a single plane appropriately outfitted can cost anywhere from $100,000 to $1.4 million. A number of people, therefore, begin by working for large aerial applications companies before they strike out on their own.

The National Agricultural Aviation Association offers job listings at its Web site, http://www.agaviation.org/content/ag-aviation-careers.

ADVANCEMENT

Agricultural pilots who work for a company can be promoted to manager. Self-employed agricultural pilots move up by charging more money for their services and increasing their client base. Another way to advance is to work in other areas of commercial aviation. These pilots may fly cargo and people to remote locations or become aerial photographers.

EARNINGS

Median annual salaries for full-time commercial pilots (a category that includes agricultural pilots) were $65,840 in 2009, according to the U.S. Department of Labor (DOL). Salaries ranged from less than $32,520 to $120,550 or more. Agricultural pilots who are employed by companies rarely get paid for vacation days and only a few companies offer health and accident insurance and profit-sharing and pension plans.

WORK ENVIRONMENT

The vast majority of an agricultural pilot's job takes place outdoors, during the early morning and early evening hours. Their work is demanding and can be hazardous. When flying, agricultural pilots wear safety gear consisting of a helmet, safety belt, and shoulder harness, because they fly under such difficult conditions. They fly close to the ground in populated areas and must be cautious to avoid obstacles. They also face exposure to pesticides and other harsh substances. When mixing or loading chemicals onto the plane, they sometimes wear gloves or masks to prevent the inhaling of harmful vapors.

OUTLOOK

Employment opportunities for experienced commercial pilots are expected to increase about as fast as the average for all occupations through 2018, according to the DOL. However, employment will not be as strong for agricultural pilots. Demand for agricultural pilots depends largely on farmers' needs. For example, during times when insect and pest control becomes a problem, there is greater demand for agricultural pilots. There is also some concern within the industry that genetically engineered crops (that are resistant to certain diseases) may decrease the need for aerial applications and cause a loss of business for agricultural pilots. Keeping these factors in mind, employment prospects will probably be best with larger farms and ranches and in states with long growing seasons.

FOR MORE INFORMATION

This organization has information on crop protection products and developments in the industry.
CropLife America
1156 15th Street, NW
Washington, DC 20005-1704
Tel: 202-296-1585
http://www.croplifeamerica.org

Visit the association's Web site to read Ag Aviation Careers: How to Become an Ag Pilot.
National Agricultural Aviation Association
1005 E Street, SE
Washington, DC 20003-2847
Tel: 202-546-5722
E-mail: information@agaviation.org
http://www.agaviation.org

For information on opportunities in the agricultural field and local chapters, contact
National FFA Organization
National FFA Center
6060 FFA Drive
PO Box 68960
Indianapolis, IN 46268-0960
Tel: 317-802-6060
https://www.ffa.org

For information on the agricultural industry, contact
U.S. Department of Agriculture
1400 Independence Avenue, SW
Washington, DC 20250-0002
Tel: 202-720-2791
http://www.usda.gov

Agricultural Scientists

QUICK FACTS

School Subjects
Agriculture
Biology
Chemistry

Personal Skills
Communication/ideas
Technical/scientific

Work Environment
Indoors and outdoors
Primarily multiple locations

Minimum Education Level
Bachelor's degree

Salary Range
$34,930 to $59,180 to
$107,670+

Certification or Licensing
Voluntary (certification)
Required for certain posi-
tions (licensing)

Outlook
Faster than the average

DOT
040, 041

GOE
02.02.02, 02.02.04

NOC
2121

O*NET-SOC
17-2021.00, 19-1012.00,
19-1013.00

OVERVIEW

Agricultural scientists study all aspects of living organisms and the relationships of plants and animals to their environment. They conduct basic research in laboratories or in the field. They apply the results to such tasks as increasing crop yields and improving the environment. Some agricultural scientists plan and administer programs for testing foods, drugs, and other products. Others direct activities at public exhibits at such places as zoos and botanical gardens. Some agricultural scientists are professors at colleges and universities or work as consultants to business firms or the government. Others work in technical sales and service jobs for manufacturers of agricultural products. There are approximately 31,000 agricultural and food scientists in the United States.

HISTORY

In 1840, Justius von Liebig of Germany published *Organic Chemistry in Its Applications to Agriculture and Physiology* and launched the systematic development of the agricultural sciences. A formal system of agricultural education soon followed in both Europe and the United States. Prior to the publication of this work, agricultural developments relied on the collective experience of farmers handed down over generations. Agricultural science has techniques in common with many other disciplines including biology, botany, genetics, nutrition, breeding, and engineering. Discoveries and improvements in these fields contributed to advances

42

in agriculture. Some milestones include the discovery of the practice of crop rotation and the application of manure as fertilizer, which greatly increased farm yields in the 1700s. Farm mechanization was greatly advanced by the invention of the mechanical reaper in 1831 and the gasoline tractor in 1892. Chemical fertilizers were first used in the 19th century; pesticides and herbicides soon followed. In 1900, the research of an Austrian monk, Gregor Johann Mendel, was rediscovered. His theories of plant characteristics, based on studies using generations of garden peas, formed the foundation for the science of genetics.

In the 20th century, scientists and engineers were at the forefront of farm, crop, and food processing improvements. Conservationist Gifford Pinchot developed some of the first methods to prevent soil erosion in 1910, and Clarence Birdseye perfected a method of freezing food in the 1920s. Birdseye's discoveries allowed for new crops of produce previously too perishable for the marketplace. Engineers in the 1930s developed more powerful farm machinery and scientists developed hybrid corn. By the 1960s, high-powered machinery and better quality feed and pesticides were in common use. Today, advances in genetic engineering and biotechnology are leading to more efficient, economical methods of farming and new markets for crops.

Agricultural scientists are also playing an important role in the development of biofuels from renewable resources such as grasses, cow dung, leftover material from crops, and corn. In the past several years, researchers have found that growing corn as a biofuel can actually be harmful to the environment. Carol Werner, executive director of the Environmental and Energy Study Institute, says that the most environmentally friendly biofuels should be made from agricultural waste products (nonedible food products) and from biomass grown on nonagricultural lands.

Another fast-growing area is the use of nanotechnology in agricultural applications. Nanotechnology is a molecular manufacturing technology that is being used to test food and agricultural products to see if they are spoiled or contaminated.

THE JOB

The nature of the work of the agricultural scientist can be broken down into several areas of specialization. Within each specialization there are various careers.

The following are careers that fall under the areas of plant and soil science.

Agronomists investigate large-scale food-crop problems, conduct experiments, and develop new methods of growing crops to ensure more efficient production, higher yields, and improved quality. They use genetic engineering to develop crops that are resistant to pests, drought, and plant diseases. They use biotechnology to increase the

An agricultural scientist *(right)* and technician collect plant samples. *(Peggy Greb, USDA, Agricultural Research Service)*

nutritional value of crops and the quality of seed stock. Agronomists also engage in soil science. They analyze soils to find ways to increase production and reduce soil erosion. They study the responses of various soil types to fertilizers, tillage practices, and crop rotation. Since soil science is related to environmental science, agronomists may also use their expertise to consult with farmers and agricultural companies on environmental quality and effective land use.

Botanists are concerned with plants and their environment, structure, heredity, and economic value in such fields as agronomy, horticulture, and medicine.

Horticulturists study fruit and nut orchards as well as garden plants such as vegetables and flowers. They conduct experiments to develop new and improved varieties and to increase crop quality and yields. They also work to improve plant culture methods for the landscaping and beautification of communities, parks, and homes.

Plant breeders apply genetics and biotechnology to improve plants' yield, quality, and resistance to harsh weather, disease, and insects. They might work on developing strains of wild or cultivated plants that will have a larger yield and increase profits.

Plant pathologists research plant diseases and the decay of plant products to identify symptoms, determine causes, and develop control measures. They attempt to predict outbreaks by studying how different soils, climates, and geography affect the spread and intensity of plant disease.

Soil scientists study the physical, chemical, and biological characteristics of soils to determine the most productive and effective planting strategies. Their research aids in producing larger, healthier crops and more environmentally sound farming procedures. (See the article Soil Scientists for more information.)

Another area of specialization for agricultural scientists is animal science.

Animal scientists conduct research and develop improved methods for housing, breeding, feeding, and controlling diseases of domestic farm animals. They inspect and grade livestock food products, purchase livestock, or work in sales and marketing of livestock products. They often consult agricultural businesses on such areas as upgrading animal housing, lowering mortality rates, or increasing production of animal products such as milk and eggs.

Dairy scientists study the selection, breeding, feeding, and management of dairy cattle. For example, they research how various types of food and environmental conditions affect milk production and quality. They also develop new breeding programs to improve dairy herds.

Poultry scientists study the breeding, feeding, and management of poultry to improve the quantity and quality of eggs and other poultry products.

Animal breeders specialize in improving the quality of farm animals. They may work for a state agricultural department, agricultural extension station, or university. Some of their work is done in a laboratory, but much of it is done outdoors working directly on animals. Using their knowledge of genetics, animal breeders develop systems for animals to achieve desired characteristics such as strength, fast maturation, resistance to disease, and quality of meat. (See the article Animal Breeders and Technicians for more information.)

Food science is a specialty closely related to animal science, but it focuses on meeting consumer demand for food products in ways that are healthy, safe, and convenient.

Food scientists use their backgrounds in chemistry, microbiology, and other sciences to develop new or better ways of preserving, packaging, processing, storing, and delivering foods. *Food technologists* work in product development to discover new food sources and analyze food content to determine levels of vitamins, fat, sugar, and protein. Food technologists also work to enforce government regulations, inspecting food-processing areas and ensuring that sanitation, safety, quality, and waste management standards are met. (See the article Food Technologists for more information.)

Another field related to agricultural science is agricultural engineering.

Agricultural engineers apply engineering principles to work in the food and agriculture industries. They design or develop agricultural equipment and machines, supervise production, and conduct tests on new designs and machine parts. They develop plans and specifications for agricultural buildings and for drainage and irrigation systems. They work on flood control, soil erosion, and land reclamation projects. They design food-processing systems and equipment to convert farm products to consumer foods. Agricultural engineers contribute to making farming easier and more profitable through the introduction of new farm machinery and through advancements in soil and water conservation. Agricultural engineers in industry engage in research or in the design, testing, or sales of equipment.

Much of the research conducted by agricultural scientists is done in laboratories and requires a familiarity with research techniques and the use of laboratory equipment and computers. Some research, however, is carried out wherever necessary. A botanist may have occasion to examine the plants that grow in the volcanic valleys of Alaska, or an animal breeder may study the behavior of animals on the plains of Africa.

REQUIREMENTS

High School
Follow your high school's college preparatory program, which will include courses in English, foreign language, mathematics, and government. Also take biology, chemistry, physics, and any other science courses available. You must also become familiar with basic computer skills, including programming. It may be possible for you to perform laboratory assistant duties for your science teachers. Visiting research laboratories and attending lectures by agricultural scientists can also be helpful.

Postsecondary Training
Educational requirements for agricultural scientists are very high. A master's degree, or more often a doctorate, is usually mandatory for careers as college or university professors, independent researchers, or field managers. A bachelor's degree may be acceptable for some entry-level jobs, such as testing or inspecting technicians, or as technical sales or service representatives. Promotions, however, are very limited for these employees unless they earn advanced degrees.

To become an agricultural scientist, you should pursue a degree related to agricultural and biological science. As an undergraduate, you should have a firm foundation in biology, with courses in chemistry, physics, mathematics, and English. Most colleges and universities have agricultural science curriculums, although liberal arts colleges may emphasize the biological sciences. State universities usually offer agricultural science programs, too.

While pursuing an advanced degree, you will participate in research projects and write a dissertation on your specialized area of study. You will also do fieldwork and laboratory research along with your classroom studies.

Certification or Licensing
The American Society of Agronomy and the Soil Science Society of America offer several certifications—including the certified crop adviser, certified professional agronomist, and certified professional soil scientist/classifier designations—to candidates based on their training and work. Contact the organizations for more information.

According to the American Society of Agricultural and Biological Engineers, agricultural engineers must hold an engineer's license.

Other Requirements

As a researcher, you should be self-motivated enough to work effectively alone, yet be able to function cooperatively as part of a team. You should have an inexhaustible curiosity about the nature of living things and their environments. You must be systematic in your work habits and in your approach to investigation and experimentation and must have the persistence to continue or start over when experiments are not immediately successful.

Work performed by agricultural scientists in offices and laboratories requires intense powers of concentration and the ability to communicate one's thoughts systematically. In addition to these skills, physical stamina is necessary for those scientists who do field research in remote areas of the world.

EXPLORING

If you live in an agricultural community, you may be able to find part-time or summer work on a farm or ranch. Joining a chapter of the National FFA Organization (formerly Future Farmers of America) or a 4-H program will introduce you to the concerns of farmers and researchers and may involve you directly in science projects. Contact your county's extension office to learn about regional projects. You may also find part-time work in veterinarian's offices, florist shops, landscape nurseries, orchards, farms, zoos, aquariums, botanical gardens, or museums. Volunteer work is often available in zoos and animal shelters.

EMPLOYERS

There are approximately 31,000 agricultural and food scientists employed in the United States. About 20 percent are employed by manufacturing companies—mainly in food and pharmaceutical manufacturing. Another 15 percent work in educational institutions. Scientists with doctorates may work on the faculty of colleges and universities. About 7 percent of all agricultural and food scientists work for the federal government. They work within the U.S. Department of Agriculture and the Environmental Protection Agency and for regional extension agencies and soil conservation departments.

STARTING OUT

Agricultural scientists often are recruited prior to graduation. College and university career services offices offer information about jobs, and students may arrange interviews with recruiters who visit the campus.

Direct application may be made to the personnel departments of colleges and universities, private industries, and nonprofit research foundations. People interested in positions with the federal government may contact the local offices of state employment services and the U.S. Office of Personnel Management (http://www.usajobs.opm. gov), which are located in various large cities throughout the country. Private employment agencies are another method that might be considered. Large companies sometimes conduct job fairs in major cities and will advertise them in the business sections of the local newspapers.

ADVANCEMENT

Advancement in this field depends on education, experience, and job performance. Agricultural scientists with advanced degrees generally start in teaching or research and advance to administrative and management positions, such as supervisor of a research program. The number of such jobs is limited, however, and often the route to advancement is through specialization. The narrower specialties are often the most valuable.

People who enter this field with only a bachelor's degree are much more restricted. After starting in testing and inspecting jobs or as technical sales and service representatives, they may progress to advanced technicians, particularly in medical research, or become high school biology teachers. In the latter case, they must have had courses in education and meet the state requirements for teaching credentials.

EARNINGS

According to the U.S. Department of Labor (DOL), the median annual salary of soil and plant scientists was approximately $59,180 in 2009. The lowest paid 10 percent (which generally included those just starting out in the field) earned less than $34,930, while the highest paid 10 percent made approximately $107,670 or more per year. Unless hired for just a short-term project, agricultural scientists most likely receive health and retirement benefits in addition to their annual salary.

WORK ENVIRONMENT

Agricultural scientists work regular hours, although researchers often choose to work longer when their experiments have reached critical points. Competition in the research field may be stiff, causing a certain amount of stress.

Agricultural scientists generally work in offices, laboratories, or classrooms where the environment is clean, healthy, and safe. Some agricultural scientists, such as botanists, periodically take field trips where living facilities may be primitive and strenuous physical activity may be required.

OUTLOOK

According to the DOL, employment for agricultural scientists is expected to grow faster than the average for all occupations through 2018. The fields of biotechnology, nanotechnology, biosecurity, genetics, and sustainable agriculture will hold the best opportunities for agricultural scientists. New developments, such as methods of processing corn and other crops for use in medicines and for fuel for motor vehicles, will alter the marketplace. Scientists will also be actively involved in improving both the environmental impact of farming and crop yields, as they focus on methods of decontaminating soil, protecting groundwater, crop rotation, and other efforts of conservation. Scientists will also have the challenge of promoting these new methods to farmers. Employment growth for animal scientists should be slightly slower than that of soil and plant scientists and food scientists and technologists.

FOR MORE INFORMATION

To learn about opportunities for scientists in the dairy industry and for information on student divisions at the college level, visit the association's Web site.

American Dairy Science Association
2441 Village Green Place
Champaign, IL 61822-7676
Tel: 217-356-5146
E-mail: adsa@assochq.org
http://www.adsa.org

To learn about careers and student competitions and scholarships, contact

American Society of Agricultural and Biological Engineers
2950 Niles Road
St. Joseph, MI 49085-8607
Tel: 269-429-0300
E-mail: hq@asabe.org
http://www.asabe.org

For information on careers and certification, contact
American Society of Agronomy
5585 Guilford Road
Madison, WI 53711-5801
Tel: 608-273-8080
https://www.agronomy.org

For information on careers, contact
Crop Science Society of America
5585 Guilford Road
Madison, WI 53711-5801
Tel: 608-273-8080
https://www.crops.org

For information on accredited food science programs and careers, visit the IFT Web site.
Institute of Food Technologists (IFT)
525 West Van Buren, Suite 1000
Chicago, IL 60607-3830
Tel: 312-782-8424
E-mail: info@ift.org
http://www.ift.org

For more information on agricultural careers and student programs, contact
National FFA Organization
6060 FFA Drive
PO Box 68960
Indianapolis, IN 46268-0960
Tel: 317-802-6060
https://www.ffa.org

For industry news and updates and general information on bio-energy, contact

Renewable Fuels Association
425 Third Street, SW, Suite 1150
Washington, DC 20024-3231
Tel: 202-289-3835
http://www.ethanolrfa.org

For information on certification and the career brochure Soils Sustain Life, *contact*
Soil Science Society of America
5585 Guilford Road
Madison, WI 53711-5801
Tel: 608-273-8080
https://www.soils.org

Visit the USDA Web site for more information on its agencies and programs as well as news releases.
U.S. Department of Agriculture (USDA)
1400 Independence Avenue, SW
Washington, DC 20250-0002
Tel: 202-720-2791
http://www.usda.gov

Animal Breeders and Technicians

OVERVIEW

Animal breeders and technicians help breed, raise, and market a variety of animals: cattle, sheep, pigs, horses, mules, and poultry for livestock; pets such as canaries, parrots, dogs, and cats; and other more exotic animals such as ostriches, alligators, minks, and many zoo animals. Technicians who are primarily involved with the breeding and feeding of animals are sometimes referred to as *animal husbandry technicians.*

In general, animal breeders and technicians are concerned with the propagation, feeding, housing, health, production, and marketing of animals. These technicians work in many different settings and capacities. They may supervise unskilled farm workers; serve as field representatives assisting in the sales of animals to customers; work in kennels, stables, ranches, or zoos reproducing species and breeds for other clients or their own organization; or work on their own on a particular breed of interest. The diversity of employment available for well-trained and well-qualified animal breeders and technicians makes this career extremely flexible. As science progresses, opportunities for these technicians should broaden. Approximately 14,700 animal breeders are employed in the United States.

QUICK FACTS

School Subjects
Biology
Business

Personal Skills
Following instructions
Technical/scientific

Work Environment
Indoors and outdoors
Primarily one location

Minimum Education Level
High school diploma

Salary Range
$18,020 to $29,680 to $60,390+

Certification or Licensing
Voluntary

Outlook
More slowly than the average

DOT
410

GOE
03.02.01

NOC
8251

O*NET-SOC
45-2021.00

HISTORY

Breeding animals has been part of raising livestock since animals were first domesticated. With the discovery of genetics, the science behind the breeding selection became more exact. Great shifts can be made in a species with genetically selected breeding programs. All domesticated dogs extend from a precursor to the modern wolf. So even though miniature poodles and St. Bernards have extremely different appearances and are seemingly incompatible, they are actually so closely related genetically that they can reproduce with each other.

Farm animals have been bred to increase meat on the animal, increase production of eggs and milk, and increase resistance to disease. Both pets and farm animals have been bred for appearance, with show animals produced in almost every domesticated species.

As regions specialized in certain breeds, organizations developed to recognize and register them, eventually developing standards for accepted breeds. Organizations such as the American Kennel Club establish criteria by which species are judged, and the criteria can be quite specific. For example, dog breeds have specific ranges of height, shoulder width, fur color, arch of leg, and such, and any dog outside the variance cannot be shown in competition. This is partly to ensure that the species is bred by trained and informed individuals, and to keep the breed from inadvertently shifting over time. Breeds, however, can be intentionally shifted, and this is how new breeds begin.

Until the end of the 20th century, breeding was controlled by reproduction through mating pairs, whether through natural or artificial insemination. Recently, however, there has been a radical breakthrough in cloning, where the gene pool of the offspring remains identical to the parent cloned. Although this work is extremely costly and experimental, it is changing the range of work that breeders can do in reproduction.

THE JOB

Most animal breeders and technicians work as *livestock production technicians* with cattle, sheep, swine, or horses; or as *poultry production technicians*, with chickens, turkeys, geese, or ducks. Other animal breeders work with domesticated animals kept as pets, such as songbirds, parrots, and all dog and cat breeds. Even wildlife populations that are kept in reserves, ranches, zoos, or aquariums are bred with the guidance of a breeder or technician. Each category of animal (such as birds), family (parrot), species (African gray parrot), and even some individual breeds within a category have technicians working on their reproduction if they are bred for livestock or domestic use. Within each of these categories the jobs may be specialized for one aspect of the animal's reproductive cycle.

On the Web

Agriculture Council of America: Careers in Agriculture
http://www.agday.org/education/careers.php

Agriculture.com
http://www.agriculture.com

USDA: Living Science: Food, Agriculture, and Natural Resources
Careers
http://www.agriculture.purdue.edu/USDA/careers

U.S. Department of Agriculture
http://www.usda.gov

For example, technicians and breeders who work in food-source bird production can be divided into specific areas of concentration. In breeding-flock production, technicians may work as *farm managers,* directing the operation of one or more farms. They may be *flock supervisors* with five or six assistants working directly with farmers under contract to produce hatching eggs. On pedigree breeding farms, technicians may oversee all the people who transport, feed, and care for the poultry. Technicians in breeding-flock production seek ways to improve efficiency in the use of time, materials, and labor; they also strive to make maximum effective use of data-processing equipment.

Technicians in hatchery management operate and maintain the incubators and hatchers, where eggs develop as embryos. These technicians must be trained in incubation, sexing, grading, scheduling, and effectively using available technology. The egg processing phase begins when the eggs leave the farm. *Egg processing technicians* handle egg pickup, trucking, delivery, and quality control. With experience, technicians in this area can work as supervisors and plant managers. These technicians need training in egg processing machinery and refrigeration equipment.

Technicians in poultry meat production oversee the production, management, and inspection of birds bred specifically for consumption as meat. Technicians may work directly with flocks or in supervisory positions.

Poultry husbandry technicians conduct research in breeding, feeding, and management of poultry. They examine selection and breeding practices in order to increase efficiency of production and to improve the quality of poultry products.

Egg candlers inspect eggs to determine quality and fitness for incubation according to prescribed standards. They check to see if eggs have been fertilized and if they are developing correctly.

Some poultry technicians also work as *field-contact technicians,* inspecting poultry farms for food-processing companies. They ensure that growers maintain contract standards for feeding and housing birds and controlling disease. They tour barns, incubation units, and related facilities to observe sanitation and weather protection provisions. Field-contact technicians ensure that specific grains are administered according to schedules, inspect birds for evidence of disease, and weigh them to determine growth rates.

For other livestock, the categories are similar, as are the range of jobs. For nonfarm animals, the average breeder works with several animals within a breed or species to produce offspring for sale. Although there are ranches that produce a large number of exotic animals and some stables and kennels that run full-staff breeding operations, most breeders for pets work out of their homes. There are also production shops, usually referred to as puppy mills, that produce pets for sale but do so without much regard to the quality or well-being of the animals they are producing. Dismissed as unprofessional by established breeders and usually challenged by local authorities for quality of care provided to the animals, these are commonly not reputable enterprises, although they may be profitable in the short term.

One area of animal production technology that merits special mention because of the increasing focus on its use in animal husbandry is that of artificial breeding. Three kinds of technicians working in this specialized area of animal production are *artificial-breeding technicians, artificial-breeding laboratory technicians,* and *artificial insemination technicians.*

Artificial breeding can be differentiated by the goal of the breeder: food (poultry and cattle), sport (horses and dogs), conservation (endangered species kept in captivity), and science (mice, rabbits, monkeys, and any other animals used for research). Breeders work to create better, stronger breeds of animals or to maintain good existing breeds.

Because of the increasing cost of shipping adult animals from location to location to keep the gene pool diverse in a species or breed, animal breeders have developed successful methods of shipping frozen semen to allow breeding across distances.

Artificial-breeding technicians collect and package semen for use in insemination. They examine the semen under a microscope to determine density and motility of sperm cells, and they dilute the semen according to standard formulas. They transfer the semen to shipping and storage containers with identifying data such as the source, date taken, and quality. They also keep records related to all of their activities. In some cases they may also be responsible for inseminating the females.

Artificial-breeding laboratory technicians handle the artificial insemination of all kinds of animals, but most often these technicians specialize in the laboratory aspects of the activity. They measure purity, potency, and density of animal semen and add extenders and antibiotics to it. They keep records, clean and sterilize laboratory equipment, and perform experimental tests to develop improved methods of processing and preserving semen.

Artificial insemination technicians do exactly what their name implies: they collect semen from the male species of an animal and artificially inseminate the female. *Poultry inseminators* collect semen from roosters and fertilize hens' eggs. They examine the roosters' semen for quality and density, measure specified amounts of semen for loading into inseminating guns, inject semen into hens, and keep accurate records of all aspects of the operation. This area of animal production is expected to grow as poultry production expands.

Whether the breeding is done artificially or naturally, the goals are the same. *Cattle breeders* mate males and females to produce animals with preferred traits such as leaner meat and less fat. It is desirable to produce cows that give birth easily and are less susceptible to illness than the average cow. In artificial insemination, cows are inseminated with a gun, much like hens, which allows for many animals to be bred from the sperm of one male. By repeating the process of artificial breeding for many generations, a more perfect animal can be produced.

Animals raised for fur or skin also require extensive technological assistance. Mink farms, ostrich farms, and alligator farms are animal production industries that need husbandry, feeding, and health technicians. As the popularity of one species rises or falls, others replace it, and new animal specialists are needed.

For all breeders, it is essential that they keep track of the lineage of the animals they breed. The genetic history for at least three previous generations is usually considered the minimum background required to ensure no inbreeding. For animals sold as pedigreed, these records are certified by some overseeing organizations. For animals being bred from wildlife stock, purity of the genetic line within a breed or species is required before an animal is allowed to reproduce. Stud books list the lineage of all animals bred within a facility. Pedigree papers travel with an individual animal as a record of that animal's lineage. Both tools are essential to breeders to keep track of the breeding programs in operation.

There are several ways to decide which animals should be bred, and some or all of them weigh into the decisions that the animal breeders make. The physical appearance and the health of the animal usually come first; this is called mass selection—where the animal is selected of its own merits. If the animal has successfully reproduced before, this is called progeny selection. The animal can be bred again, knowing that the animal has produced desirable offspring previously. However, if that particular animal becomes genetically overrepresented in a generation, then the breeder runs the risk of inbreeding with the generations to follow. So the value of that animal's offspring has to be weighed against the need for diversity in parents. Family selection also determines the value of reproducing an animal. Some genetic diversity can come from breeding siblings of a good breeder, but it may not be enough diversity if the breeder is working with a limited stock of animals. Pedigree is the final determiner in evaluating a breeding animal.

REQUIREMENTS

High School
High school students seeking to enter this field will find that the more agriculture and science courses they select in high school, the better prepared they will be. In addition, courses in mathematics, business, communications, chemistry, and mechanics are valuable.

Postsecondary Training
Nine months to two years at a technical school or a college diploma are the usual minimum credentials for animal breeders and technicians. Many colleges now offer two- and four-year programs in animal science or animal husbandry where additional knowledge, skills, and specialized training may be acquired. Besides learning the scientific side of animal breeding, including instruction in genetics, animal physiology, and some veterinary science, students also take business classes that help them see the field from an economic point of view. With the increasing use of technology for breeding livestock and domesticated nonfarm animals, a bachelor's degree becomes more important for succeeding in the field. Master's and doctoral degrees are useful for the most specialized fields and the careers that require the most sophisticated genetic planning. Higher degrees are

required for potential teachers in the field, and the current work being done in cloning is done exclusively by people with doctorates.

Whether trained by experience, at an academic institution, or both, all new hires at major breeding companies are usually put through some type of training program.

Certification or Licensing
Certification is not required, but nearly all major companies have certification programs that can enhance earnings and opportunities.

Other Requirements
Animal breeders and technicians should have great love, empathy, and respect for animals. You must be patient and compassionate in addition to being very knowledgeable about the needs and habits of all the animals in your care. You must also have interest in reproductive science, genetics, and animal physiology. It is important to be able to communicate easily with agricultural scientists, farmers, and other animal owners and caretakers.

EXPLORING

Organizations such as 4-H Clubs (http://www.4-h.org) and the National FFA Organization (formerly known as Future Farmers of America, https://www.ffa.org) offer good opportunities for hearing about, visiting, and participating in farm activities. Programs sponsored by 4-H allow students to learn firsthand about breeding small animals for show.

Other opportunities might include volunteering at a breeding farm or ranch, kennel, or stable where animals are bred and sold. This will give you a chance to see the work required and begin to get experience in practical skills for the job.

For at-home experience, raising pets is a good introduction to the skills needed in basic animal maintenance. Learning how to care for, feed, and house a pet provides some basic knowledge of working with animals. In addition, you can learn more about this field by reading books on animals and their care. But unless you have background and experience in breeding, and a good mentor to work with, it is not recommended that you start breeding your pet. There are literally millions of unwanted dogs and cats that come from mixed breeds or unpedigreed purebreds, and many of these animals are destroyed because there are no homes for them.

Other opportunities that provide animal maintenance experience include volunteering to work at animal shelters, veterinary offices, and pet breeders' businesses.

EMPLOYERS

Approximately 14,700 animal breeders are employed in the United States. Animal breeders and technicians used to work for themselves, but today most are employed by corporate breeders. A few may still own their own livestock ranches, and some do it only as a sideline or hobby.

STARTING OUT

Many junior colleges participate in "learn-and-earn" programs, in which the college and prospective employer jointly provide the student's training, both in the classroom and through on-the-job work with livestock and other animals. Most technical programs offer placement services for graduates, and the demand for qualified people often exceeds the supply.

ADVANCEMENT

Even when a good training or technical program is completed, the graduate often must begin work at a low level before advancing to positions with more responsibility. But the technical program graduate will advance much more rapidly to positions of major responsibility and greater financial reward than the untrained worker.

Those graduates willing to work hard and keep abreast of changes in their field may advance to livestock breeder, feedlot manager, supervisor, or artificial breeding distributor. If they have the necessary capital, they can own their own livestock ranches.

EARNINGS

Salaries vary widely depending on employer, the technicians' educational and agricultural background, the kind of animal the technicians work with, and the geographical areas in which they work. In general, the salaries of breeders tend to be higher in areas with a heavy concentration and in the breeding of certain specialty animals. Kentucky, for instance, leads the nation in the breeding of horses, and, unsurprisingly, that is where salaries are highest. The U.S. Department of Labor (DOL) reports that animal breeders earned median annual wages of $29,680 in 2009. The top paid 10 percent made $60,390 or more, while the bottom paid 10 percent made $18,020 or less. Fringe benefits vary according to employer but can include paid vacation time, health insurance, and pension benefits.

WORK ENVIRONMENT

Working conditions vary from operation to operation, but certain factors always exist. Much of the work is done inside in all types of facilities. Barns, pens, and stables are the most common facilities for farm animals; nonfarm animals may be bred in private homes or housing facilities. Both types of work often require long, irregular hours and work on weekends and holidays. The work is also sometimes dangerous, especially when large animals such as stallions and bulls are involved. Salaries are usually commensurate with the hours worked, and there are usually slack seasons when time off is given to compensate any extra hours worked. But for people with a strong desire to work with animals, long working hours or other less desirable conditions are offset by the benefits of this career.

Animal breeders and technicians are often their own bosses and make their own decisions. While this can be an asset to those who value independence, prospective animal breeders and technicians must realize that self-discipline is the most valuable trait for success.

OUTLOOK

Employment for animal breeders is expected to grow more slowly than the average for all careers through 2018, according to the DOL. Continuing changes are expected in the next few years, in both the production and the marketing phases of the animal production industry. Because of the costs involved, it is almost impossible for a one-person operation to stay in business for farm animals. As a result, cooperatives of consultants and corporations will become more prevalent with greater emphasis placed on specialization. This, in turn, will increase the demand for technical program graduates. Other factors, such as small profit margins, the demand for more uniform products, and an increasing foreign market, will result in a need for more specially trained personnel. This is a new era of specialization in the animal production industry; graduates of animal production technology programs have an interesting and rewarding future ahead of them.

FOR MORE INFORMATION

For information on careers and graduate programs, contact
American Society of Animal Science
2441 Village Green Place
Champaign, IL 61822-7676
Tel: 217-356-9050
E-mail: asas@assochq.org
http://www.asas.org

For industry information, contact
National Cattlemen's Beef Association
9110 East Nichols Avenue, #300
Centennial, CO 80112-3425
Tel: 303-694-0305
http://www.beef.org

For information on the agricultural industry, contact
U.S. Department of Agriculture
1400 Independence Avenue, SW
Washington, DC 20250-0002
Tel: 202-720-2791
http://www.usda.gov

Aquaculturists

OVERVIEW

Aquaculturists, also known as *aquacultural managers, fish farmers, fish culturists,* or *mariculturists,* raise fish, shellfish, or other aquatic life (such as aquatic plants) under controlled conditions for profit and/or human consumption.

HISTORY

The roots of fish farming go far back in history. Fish culturing began in at least 1000 B.C., possibly even earlier in Egypt and China. Ancient China introduced ornamental-goldfish breeding to Japan, which in turn developed ornamental-carp breeding. Ancient Romans were the first mariculturists, creating ponds for fish breeding that let in ocean water. Brackish-water fish farms existed in Java by about 1400 A.D. However, historically, the vast majority of food-fish has come from capture, not farming. Capture fishery worldwide grew at rates of about 4 percent per year through most of the 20th century but increased by only 0.6 percent between 1986 and 1987 (to about 93 million metric tons). Since then, growth rates of less than 1 percent per year have been the norm. In a nutshell, the natural supply of fish is shrinking—natural waters are being "fished out"—while fish consumption is rising. Enter aquaculture.

U.S. aquaculture began in the 1920s and 1930s with some farming of minnows for bait and with the growth of catfish, bass, and other food-fish farming in the 1950s, largely in the South. In 1975, U.S. aquaculture produced 130 million pounds of fish; by 2007, it produced nearly 566 million pounds. Today, U.S. aquaculture produces

QUICK FACTS

School Subjects
Biology
Business

Personal Skills
Mechanical/manipulative
Technical/scientific

Work Environment
Indoors and outdoors
Primarily one location

Minimum Education Level
Bachelor's degree

Salary Range
$16,700 to $43,570 to $103,210+

Certification or Licensing
Required by certain states

Outlook
Faster than the average

DOT
446

GOE
03.01.01

NOC
2221, 8257, 8613

O*NET-SOC
11-9011.00, 11-9011.03,
45-1011.06, 45-2099.00,
45-3011.00

catfish, crawfish, salmon, trout, oysters, ornamental fish, and other products. U.S. restaurants offer a wide range of fish and other organisms produced by aquaculture, including salmon, shrimp, catfish, crabs, clams, mussels, lobster, carp, sturgeon, cod, and mahi-mahi (dolphin). As capture yields have leveled off, aquaculture yields have grown. In fact, aquaculture production grew by 11.7 percent from 1998 to 2005. Today, aquaculture is a nearly $1.1 billion annual industry in the United States. Aquaculture now accounts for 50 percent of the fish consumed globally, according to the *Proceedings of the National Academy of Sciences.*

Some hope aquaculture can help meet food needs in developing countries. Fish is a healthier source of protein than meat and requires less energy to produce (about two pounds of feed for one pound of catfish, versus eight pounds of feed for one pound of beef). Aquaculture can still be done simply and cheaply, such as in a pond, using farm waste as fertilizer. (Such setups, however, produce less desirable fish, like carp.)

THE JOB

The term aquaculturist typically is used to describe someone who raises fish for profit. This is not a conservation job; while aquaculturists may have a degree in fisheries biology or other fish science, just like some of the people working for the U.S. Fish and Wildlife Service, the Biological Resources Discipline of the U.S. Geological Survey, other federal agencies, or for federal or state fish hatcheries, they do not share those agencies' goal of protecting rare and endangered species.

Technically speaking, aquaculture can be done in fresh water, brackish (salty or somewhat salty) water, seawater, flooded fields, rice paddies, and other waters. Practically speaking, limited areas in the United States are appropriate for aquaculture. Right now, U.S. aquaculture is focused in the South (catfish), the West (salmon), and a few other areas (like bait farms in Arkansas). There must be markets for the products, capital to develop the site, appropriate water supplies, and proper structures for handling effluent. Conditions must be right; for example, catfish production in the South is successful because of the warmer waters, longer growing season, and other factors. Fish farms range in size from a few acres to 50 acres or more and typically focus on one type of fish (such as trout or catfish) or shellfish (such as clams, shrimp, or oysters). Rearing may be done in earth ponds, concrete ponds, or pens in seas, lakes, or ocean waters.

Fish farming differs significantly from regular farming. Raising fish is more complicated because of their environment—water. Also, intensely confined animals tend to be more susceptible to disease; many of these fish are in a confined space. Raising fish is more like a feedlot raising penned animals than a rancher raising cattle in open rangelands. The raising of fish also requires closer monitoring than raising farm animals.

A primary goal of aquaculture is to increase fish production beyond what's possible in nature. In recent years, there's been a lot of research to determine which fish are most suited to fish farming, what to feed them and in what quantities, what conditions will optimize production and quality, and other areas. Biologists and other research scientists have experimented with things like crossbreeding for better genetics (such as for increased egg production). Commercial feeds and supplements have been developed to boost fish size. Aquaculturists also have been working on least-cost feeding formulas, or ratios of lowest costing food to highest quantity and quality fish, for better profits. Experiments with the effects of light on growth, with limiting feeding, and other research studies also have been conducted. Since confined fish may be more susceptible to diseases, researchers also have developed drugs such as fluoroquinolone for FDA approval.

In fish farming, eggs are stripped from the female fish, fertilized by milt from the male fish, and placed in moist pans or hatchery trays. These are put in incubators to spawn the eggs. Resulting fingerlings are put in the rearing ponds or other waters for further growth. They may be fed high-protein food or cereal with vitamins

Sea Grant Association

The Sea Grant Association (http://www.sga.seagrant.org) offers funding to colleges and universities to support the understanding, use, and conservation of marine and coastal resources. Some recently funded projects include studies on

- how to prevent oyster disease in Chesapeake Bay
- the spawning of flounder in fish farms in North Carolina
- how to minimize water use and waste water discharge on fish farms
- how to breed striped bass year-round in captivity
- sustainable coastal development.

or minerals so they will achieve good size and quality. Aquaculturists also monitor water quality, add drugs to fight disease, and otherwise optimize growing conditions. Once the right size is reached, which can take up to three years or more, the fish are removed from the water, counted, weighed, and loaded into a truck or dressed and packed in ice for shipment to the buyer.

In shellfish farming, clams, oysters, and other shellfish are cultivated in specially prepared beds near the shoreline and then harvested. Tide flats are laid out and dikes created to control water drainage at low tide. The spawn of oysters or other shellfish, known as spat, are sown in the beds and may be covered with sand or broken shells. When the tide is up and the beds are covered with water, the beds may be dragged with nets to remove crabs, starfish, or other predators. At low tide, workers walk into the bed and collect full-grown shellfish for packing and sale.

Positions within the fish farm operation may include a manager or superintendent, supervisors, and workers. A manager or superintendent heads the operation, helping to establish policies and procedures and conferring with biologists or other scientists on optimal feeding and other conditions. They also may handle hiring, firing, payroll, and other personnel matters; monitor budgets and costs; and do other administrative work. Supervisors oversee the spawning, rearing, harvesting, and other day-to-day farming activities. They might train workers, prepare reports, and help monitor quality control. Workers may be called assistants, attendants, bed workers, or similar titles, and they do the labor-intensive parts of the fish farming operation.

Scientists working within the fish farming operation, or in research facilities supporting aquaculture, include *fisheries biologists* and *harvest management biologists*. They focus on fish living habits, relationships, growth, rearing, stocking, and the like.

Some aquaculturists work in universities trying to find ways to improve aquaculture production. For example, experiments done at Auburn University's aquaculture center have shown that limiting feed actually can increase fish weight and protein amount. Researchers and economists also have developed feasibility studies, focusing on the potential viability of different types of aquaculture for various regions. For example, a 1994 University of Florida study said tropical fish, aquatic plants, and bait-fish might be the future of aquaculture in that state, rather than catfish farming. Research goes on worldwide; for example, in 1995 the Institute of Aquaculture in Scotland studied the use of immune system stimulants to encourage macrophage growth in fish.

An aquaculturist checks on the number of baby fish being loaded on a transport truck. *(Rogelio V. Solis, AP Photo)*

REQUIREMENTS

High School

Most jobs in aquaculture require a bachelor's degree, so follow a college preparatory plan of English, history, government, foreign language, and other courses recommended by your school counselor. Take science courses, particularly biology courses, to prepare for a marine science, aquaculture, or biology college program. Some management experience is also important, so take courses in business and accounting.

Postsecondary Training

A bachelor's degree is the minimum requirement for jobs in aquaculture beyond the laborer or assistant level. Researchers usually have an advanced degree in their specialty. Jobs in aquaculture tend to be more plentiful than jobs with fish and wildlife management agencies (which are very tough to get), but the educational requirements are basically the same. Without a bachelor's degree, it is very difficult to find work at the professional level. In part, fish farming is more complicated today, given new understanding of ecology (such as how one organism impacts another), fish genetics (such as how fish adapt themselves genetically to a natural environment), and other areas. A bachelor's degree in fish and wildlife biology is the primary path into this field. A minor in business or accounting may also be valuable to a prospective aquaculturist. The World Aquaculture Society offers a list of postsecondary aquaculture and related training programs at its Web site, https://www.was.org.

Certification or Licensing

The American Fisheries Society offers certification to fishery science professionals. A certain number of hours of work and educational experience plus a written test are necessary. Both private and government fish people obtain these certifications. In some areas, they are required for obtaining some positions and for receiving raises and promotions.

Other Requirements

You should be people-oriented because you'll often work with private market suppliers, the public, and politicians. Good writing skills will come in handy in some positions, as will business and administrative skills like budgeting. A knowledge of computer modeling and statistics can help in newer areas like harvest management and population dynamics.

EXPLORING

Contact the American Fisheries Society for information about careers in aquaculture. Also, read *Aquaculture North America* and visit its Web site (http://aquaculturenorthamerica.com) to learn more about the issues of the industry. Any hands-on experience you can get, even in high school, will be helpful in landing a job. Through a "shadowing" project, you may be able to spend some time in a local hatchery at the side of an aquaculturist. Volunteering at one of the approximately 70 federal fish hatcheries nationwide, or a state hatchery, is an option. Contact local hatcheries, go meet the people there, and find out about applying for a job. Experience at a pet shop that sells different varieties of saltwater fish, or at a state aquarium, can also give you insight into the industry.

EMPLOYERS

Aquaculturists can find work with commercial and private fish farms owned by corporations, states, or individuals. They may work with a small family-run operation or with a large operation employing hundreds of people. According to a recent survey by the U.S. Department of Agriculture (USDA), the top five producing states by value are Mississippi, Arkansas, Florida, Maine, and Alabama. The USDA also reports that 68 percent of the fish farms are located in the southern United States. Facilities, however, range across the country and include rainbow trout farms in Idaho, oyster farms in Washington State, and salmon farms in Maine. Some universities also hire aquaculturists, as do the U.S. Fish and Wildlife Service, and other national organizations.

STARTING OUT

Aquaculture work usually is easier to find than fishery or wildlife agency work, but it can't hurt to follow some of the same strategies used to land those jobs: namely, get experience. Become a student chapter member of the American Fisheries Society and explore this group's national job listings. Work with your university's career services office. A person looking for a job needs to be pretty flexible. Since U.S. aquaculture is more developed in some areas, such as the South and West, your first job may take you to a new region.

International opportunities are possible, too. Those who have considered the Peace Corps should know that some volunteers work in aquaculture. (Peace Corps volunteers must be U.S. citizens and at least 18 years old; those with a college education or at least three years' experience in their specialty have a better chance of being accepted into the program.) Groups like UNICEF and the U.S. Agency for International Development also use fish and wildlife specialists.

Beyond these types of organizations, other international job opportunities may be possible wherever aquaculture is practiced. Scandinavians raise a lot of coldwater fish; the Japanese raise shellfish, algae, and kelp. Of course, pollution has made some fresh waters in Europe, like the Thames in England, unsuitable for fish farming activities.

ADVANCEMENT

In fish farming, the professional typically enters as a fish biologist or other fish scientist and advances to some kind of manager or supervisor position. As noted earlier, state certification may help speed this process in some areas. Fish farming is a business; each operation is different, but further raises or promotions are likely to hinge on profits, customer satisfaction, development and sustaining of new markets, and similar business successes. On the research side, advancement will depend on the individual employer. With a young U.S. aquaculture industry clamoring for information, new research and development, and improved aquaculture technologies, it's possible for fish scientists in research to have a big impact with their studies and reap the financial benefits of doing so.

EARNINGS

Earnings in aquaculture can vary greatly. Aquaculture farms employ graduate students in assistantships, as well as experienced professionals with Ph.D.'s in genetics. Entry-level technicians may begin at $8 an hour; those with a great deal of experience and a degree may begin at a salary of $35,000 a year. The National Association of Colleges and Employers estimates that biologists with bachelor's degrees, working in private industry in 2009, had a starting wage of $33,254 a year.

The U.S. Department of Labor reports that agricultural workers, including aquaculture professionals, had median annual earnings of $25,610 in 2009. Annual salaries ranged from less than $16,700 to more than $43,570. Salaries for agricultural managers ranged from less than $31,680 to $103,210 or more.

Benefits for full-time workers include vacation and sick time, health, and sometimes dental, insurance, and pension or 401(k) plans.

WORK ENVIRONMENT

A fish farm is not much different from a mink farm or other operation aimed at raising high volumes of animals. Those who don't like that idea should think twice about this career. On the other hand, fish farms and fish hatcheries give aquaculturists the opportunity to work outdoors, to apply scientific education in a concrete way, and to make a difference in a young and growing industry. Some fish farm operations are small, and some are large; trout farming, for example, is made up of both small and large operations. This variety allows workers in the field to find the size and style of operation that's right for them.

Fishery and wildlife careers sound romantic, and in some ways, they are; that's why they're so popular. Much of the work of an aquaculturist, however, is very pragmatic, including fighting fish diseases.

People drawn to fishery and wildlife management tend to like the outdoors. This work also involves frequent interaction with others, and the successful aquaculturist should have good people skills.

OUTLOOK

The outlook for the U.S. aquaculture industry is promising. A subcommittee of the U.S. Department of Commerce predicts there will be a 70 percent increase in world seafood demand by 2025. Commercial fisheries are overharvested, so much of this demand will be met by aquaculture. Aquaculture's ability to meet this demand, however, will depend on the growth and development of the industry. Many universities are currently benefiting from grants that allow them to explore better methods of growing and harvesting product and preventing disease. Advances in these areas will help to lower risk and increase profits, attracting more interest in the industry.

FOR MORE INFORMATION

For information about certification, educational programs, and the professional society serving fisheries scientists, contact
American Fisheries Society
5410 Grosvenor Lane
Bethesda, MD 20814-2199
Tel: 301-897-8616

http://www.fisheries.org

For information on the agricultural industry, contact
U.S. Department of Agriculture
1400 Independence Avenue, SW
Washington, DC 20250-0002
Tel: 202-720-2791
http://www.usda.gov

For information about college programs, industry journals, publications, membership, and job postings, contact
World Aquaculture Society (U.S. Branch)
143 J. M. Parker Coliseum
Louisiana State University
Baton Rouge, LA 70803-0001
Tel: 225-578-3137
E-mail: wasmas@aol.com
http://www.was.org

This Web site provides information and links to state, national, and international aquaculture resources.
Aquaculture Network Information Center
http://aquanic.org

Beekeepers

OVERVIEW

Beekeepers, also known as *apiarists,* care for and raise honeybees for commercial and agricultural purposes, such as honey production and crop pollination. Their duties might include assembling beehives and other equipment, buying and selling bees, establishing settlements close to pollination-dependent crops, transporting wild beehives to a central location, raising queen bees, and harvesting and selling honey. Beekeepers may work on farms or small plots of land to raise bees to assist in the production of grain and other agricultural crops. It is said that one-third of food production in the United States depends on bees. Beekeeping may be a full-time job, a "sideline" job, or a hobby. Beekeepers usually work alone or as a member of a small team.

HISTORY

Early rock paintings in Spain and Africa depict people gathering honey from trees or rock crevices while bees flew around them. Ancient Egyptian relics show the beekeeper taking honey from a hive while a helper drives the bees away with smoke. There is evidence that the Mayans kept a stingless, honey-storing bee. Relics from Belize and Mexico, including stone disks thought to have been the end stoppers on wooden log-shaped hives, represent the oldest artifacts related to beekeeping in the New World.

Early honey gatherers probably accidentally discovered that smoke calms bees when they used fire to drive off other animals. Beekeeping may have originally developed following the observation that swarms of bees will settle in any container with a dark,

QUICK FACTS

School Subjects
Agriculture
Biology
Earth science

Personal Skills
Mechanical/manipulative
Technical/scientific

Work Environment
Primarily outdoors
One location with some
 travel

Minimum Education Level
Apprenticeship

Salary Range
$0 to $10,000 to $20,000+

Certification or Licensing
Required by certain states

Outlook
Decline

DOT
413

GOE
N/A

NOC
8251

O*NET-SOC
11-9012.00

protected interior space. Pottery and natural containers, such as holes in trees or logs, provide shelter and protection for hive establishment. In some forested areas of Europe, hive clusters made from logs can still be found. Horizontal pottery hives are used along the Mediterranean, and straw hives, known as "skeps," are still used in Belgium and France.

The honeybee, which is not native to North America, was shipped to the colonies from England in the first half of the 17th century. For many years, straw skeps were used for hives, followed by log "gums." With these crude hives, it was difficult to know when the bees had problems with disease or starvation or if they were queenless; the beekeeper could not inspect the combs to determine what was wrong. By the same token, it was difficult to extract honey from these hives without damaging or destroying the bee colony. Typically, beekeepers had to kill their swarms each fall by burning sulphur at the entrance of the hive; then the honey and beeswax could be removed.

In the 17th and 18th centuries, beekeepers began to build movable-comb hives, which enabled them to inspect combs without damaging them. In 1789, Francis Huber invented the first movable-frame hive. The combs in this hive could be easily inspected like the pages of a book. In 1852, Lorenzo Langstroth, a minister from Pennsylvania, patented a hive with movable frames that hung from the top of the hive, leaving a 3/8-inch space between the frames and the hive body (the exact spacing at which bees will build comb they can move around, referred to today as "beespace"). By the turn of the 20th century, most beekeepers were using Langstroth's system. Langstroth is known as "the father of modern beekeeping."

Modern beekeeping methods evolved very rapidly following the invention of Langstroth's system. Wax-comb foundation, which made possible the consistent production of high-quality combs of worker cells, was invented in 1857. The centrifugal honey extractor was invented in 1865, enabling large-scale production of honey, and later in the century the radial extractor (where both sides of the frame are extracted at the same time) was invented. In 1889, G. M. Doolittle of New York developed the system for rearing queen bees that is still used today by all commercial queen-rearers. Bee smokers and veils evolved and improved. Also around this time, leaders in American beekeeping learned of the merits of the Italian honeybee, and they began to import these bees into the states. Today, the American version of the Italian honeybee is still widely used throughout the country.

Top Honey-Producing States by Production, 2008

1. North Dakota
2. South Dakota
3. California
4. Florida
5. Minnesota
6. Montana
7. Michigan
8. Texas
9. Wisconsin
10. Georgia

Source: National Agricultural Statistics Service

The most significant advances in beekeeping today are related to the areas of bee management and the extracting process. In general, the dimensions of hives and frames have become more standardized, drugs are available for disease control, artificial insemination of queen bees is being used commercially, and colony rental is being used increasingly for crop pollination. According to the National Honey Board, approximately 2.5 million colonies are rented for pollination annually.

In recent years, the commercial U.S. beekeeping industry has faced many challenges—ranging from the decimation of honeybee colonies by Colony Collapse Disorder and other diseases to foreign competitors that offer honey and orchard pollination services that are much less expensive than those offered by U.S. beekeepers.

THE JOB

In the spring, beekeepers set up new hives and repair old ones. A beginning beekeeper will have to purchase bees from a dealer. The beekeeper will set up the hive near an orchard or field where nectar will be available for the bees.

A beekeeper's primary task is the care and feeding of the bees. The hives must be inspected regularly for mite infestations and diseases.

The bees must also occasionally be fed, especially during the winter months when forage is unavailable.

Beekeepers ensure that the bees and their surroundings are healthy and clean. They watch out for robber bees, who will try to rob food from other hives when they are unable to find enough nectar to make honey. Beekeepers make it easier for the bees to defend the hive by limiting the size of the entrance. Beekeepers must also watch for "swarming," a situation in which about half of the bees from a colony look for a new place to live because the hive has become too crowded or is no longer adequately ventilated. To prevent swarming, the entrance to the hive can be enlarged to improve air circulation, especially during the summer. The bee-keeper might also clip the queen's wing to prevent her from leaving with the swarm or move half the bees to a new hive with another queen.

The queen bee also requires special attention. In a properly func-tioning hive, the queen will be almost constantly laying eggs. If she becomes sick or old, the beekeeper will need to replace her.

Beekeepers must wear special equipment when working with bees. A veil and plastic helmet protect the beekeeper's head and neck from the stings of angry bees. Some beekeepers also wear thick clothing and gloves for protection, although many profession-

A beekeeper checks honey production at his bee farm. (*Imaginechina/ AP Photo*)

als feel that the thick clothes are too bulky and hot. Their choice is to risk the occasional sting to gain the benefit of wearing lighter clothing.

A beekeeper uses smoke to keep the bees from swarming in anger. An angry bee gives off a scent that alarms the rest of the hive. Smoke, produced in a special smoker device, masks the alarm scent, preventing the formation of an attack swarm.

Beekeepers must purchase or construct special enclosures to contain the beehives. The most popular model in the United States is the Langstroth hive, a rectangular wood and metal construction that sits upon a stand to keep it dry.

Harvesting honey is an important part of the beekeeper's job. When the honey is ready for harvesting, beekeepers seal the honeycomb with beeswax. They remove the frames of honeycombs and take them to the extractor, where the honey is spun out of the honeycomb. It is filtered and drained into a tank. The honey is stored in five-gallon buckets or in 55-gallon drums. This is a part of beekeeping where physical strength is important.

Beekeepers also spend time keeping data on their colonies. Their records track information regarding the queens, any extra food that may have been required, honey yields and dates, and so forth.

REQUIREMENTS

High School

If you're interested in beekeeping, you should take high school classes in business and mathematics to prepare you for the records-keeping aspect of this work. Science classes, such as natural sciences, biology, and earth science, will give you an understanding of the environment as well as processes such as pollination. If your high school offers agriculture classes, be sure to take those for added understanding of crop and animal production. Wood shop classes will also be useful if you intend to build your own hives.

Postsecondary Training

Many people learn to do this work by getting informal on-the-job training when working with an experienced beekeeper. Community or junior colleges that offer agriculture classes may also provide another avenue for learning about honey production and bee care. Finally, some states may offer apprenticeship programs in beekeeping. To find out what agency to contact in your state regarding apprenticeships, visit the Employment and Training Administration's Web site at http://www.doleta.gov.

Certification or Licensing

Beekeeping licenses are issued at the state level, and requirements vary from state to state. Some states do not require a license at all, although almost every state requires that the commercial beekeeper register every hive.

Other Requirements

While a love of nature and the ability and desire to work alone were once among the most important characteristics for a beekeeper, many beekeepers today feel that a shrewd business sense and marketing savvy are what's most necessary to survive. Most commercial beekeepers seem to agree that the key to success as a beekeeper lies less in working with the bees than in working in the commercial business marketplace. Therefore, a good understanding of economics and basic business accounting is essential to the practice of beekeeping.

Nevertheless, beekeepers still need physical strength, endurance, and a love of the outdoors to be successful. Of course, a beekeeper will also be working with large groups of insects, so this is not a job for people with aversions to insects or allergies to bee venom.

EXPLORING

If you are interested in beekeeping, you should contact a local beekeeping association for advice and guidance. You should find an experienced, successful beekeeper who is willing to share his or her knowledge. A part-time job with a beekeeper would be an ideal introduction to the trade, but the opportunity simply to observe a beekeeper and ask questions is also invaluable. Read as much as you can about beekeeping. Start by checking out your local library for books on the subject; look for books written specifically for your part of the country. You should also subscribe to a beekeeping magazine, such as *Bee Culture* (http://www.beeculture.com) or *American Bee Journal* (http://www.americanbeejournal.com). Join a local chapter of 4-H or the National FFA (formerly Future Farmers of America). While you may not gain direct experience with beekeeping, you will be able to work on agricultural or other projects and gain management experience.

EMPLOYERS

Beekeeping is a small and specialized profession. The National Honey Board estimates that there are approximately 1,600 commercial beekeeping operations in the United States (defined as those with 300 or more bee colonies). The vast majority of beekeepers today do not depend on beekeeping for their income; they're known in the trade as "sideliners" or hobbyists. Most beekeepers run their own independent business rather than work for a large commercial establishment.

STARTING OUT

Since most beekeepers work independently, the most likely route of entry is to learn the basics and invest in some starting equipment. You can contact your local beekeeping association for advice. Keep in mind that if you hope to raise bees for commercial profit, you will need a substantial amount of capital to get started, and you're likely to face several years without profits while you work to increase honey production. If you live in an area where bees are raised, you should contact local beekeepers who may hire you for part-time or seasonal work.

ADVANCEMENT

Advancement in this field most often comes as beekeepers increase the number of hives they own and increase their commercial sales. It isn't likely that new beekeepers will be able to support themselves by beekeeping alone; most likely it will be a hobby or a sideline to supplement their living.

EARNINGS

Earnings for beekeepers vary greatly, even from year to year, as honey prices fluctuate and production from hives changes. Other variables that affect earnings include the number of hives a beekeeper has, the type of honey produced, and the season's weather conditions. Some beekeepers end up with no profits. Commercial beekeepers may only make in the $10,000 to $20,000 range. The National Agricultural Statistics Service reports the average price paid for the honey crop was approximately $1.41 per pound in 2008, and colonies averaged a production of 69.9 pounds. This means that a beekeeper could potentially earn $98.56 from every colony owned. Remember, however, expenses and taxes have not been subtracted from this amount. To make a profit, a beekeeper typically needs to have thousands of colonies producing well. Medium- and small-sized operations usually have a difficult time turning any profit.

Some beekeepers are able to earn income through raising hives to rent to crop growers. Rental fees vary, but it's not unusual for a beekeeper in California to get $136 per colony for a two- to four-week period during the almond-growing season. Some small-scale beekeepers are able to market and sell specialty items (for example, beeswax-based products) that can be profitable, but again, this is usually a hobby or sideline, not an exclusive source of income.

Since beekeepers usually run their own businesses, they generally do not have paid sick days or holidays. In addition, they are typically responsible for providing their own insurance and retirement plans. Beekeepers who are salaried employees receive fringe benefits.

WORK ENVIRONMENT

Beekeepers work primarily outdoors. The "in-season" hours (mostly in the spring and summer) can be very long, and the work can be physically challenging. Those who enjoy nature might well be suited for beekeeping, but there are indoor components to the work as well, such as tending to business records, processing honey, and caring for equipment. This is a field that requires discipline and the ability to work without supervision. A beekeeper must spend many hours working alone in tasks that can be grueling. Many beekeepers work part time at the trade while performing other agricultural duties. Those with a sensitivity to bee stings should certainly avoid this industry, as—despite protective gear—stings are an inevitable part of the job.

OUTLOOK

With approximately 1,600 commercial beekeepers currently in operation in the United States and one-third of our food supply dependent on honeybees for pollination, it might seem logical to assume that there will be increasing demand for the services of beekeepers in the future. But foreign competition and an increase in bee diseases are strongly affecting employment opportunities for beekeepers. Foreign pollination service companies are now competing with U.S.-based companies for business at U.S. farms. And although honey prices have recently hit record highs, it is still difficult for U.S. beekeepers to compete with foreign imports in terms of price. Foreign honey producers have fewer environmental regulations to abide by, lower wage rates to pay, and fewer worker benefits to provide. Thus, they are able to charge less for their product. Additionally, Colony Collapse Disorder, which is characterized by sudden colony death, has decimated honeybee colonies across the United States. Although demand for commercial pollination services has risen in recent years (especially in California as a result of the increase in almond growing), beekeepers are finding it harder to raise and care for healthy bees to provide these services.

Despite the weak employment outlook, many people will continue to keep bees as a hobby or sideline business.

FOR MORE INFORMATION

For career information and statistics on beekeeping, contact
Agricultural Marketing Resource Center
Iowa State University
1111 NSRIC
Ames, IA 50011-3310
Tel: 866-277-5567
E-mail: AgMRC@iastate.edu
http://www.agmrc.org

The American Beekeeping Federation acts on behalf of the beekeeping industry on issues affecting the interests and the economic viability of the various sectors of the industry. The organization offers a free beginning beekeeping information packet, sponsors an essay contest in conjunction with 4-H and also has a Honey Queen and Honey Princess Program. For more information, contact
American Beekeeping Federation
3525 Piedmont Road, Building 5, Suite 300
Atlanta, GA 30305-1578
Tel: 404-760-2875
E-mail: info@abfnet.org
http://www.abfnet.org

The Back Yard Beekeepers Association is a national club that provides their membership with interesting and practical information about the "how-to's" of beekeeping. The club also provides the general public with educational programs about honeybees and the benefits of beekeeping in the community. Visit its Web site to locate a club near you.
Back Yard Beekeepers Association
http://www.backyardbeekeepers.com

For information on the programs offered by these organizations and how to join, contact

National 4-H Headquarters
U.S. Department of Agriculture
National Institute of Food and Agriculture
1400 Independence Avenue, SW, Stop 2225
Washington, DC 20250-2225
Tel: 202-401-4114
E-mail: 4hhq@nifa.usda.gov
http://www.national4-hheadquarters.gov and http://4-h.org

National FFA Organization
6060 FFA Drive
PO Box 68960
Indianapolis, IN 46268-0960
Tel: 317-802-6060
https://www.ffa.org

The National Honey Board serves the honey industry by increasing demand for honey and honey products. Check out its Web site for information on the industry.
National Honey Board
11409 Business Park Circle, Suite 210
Firestone, CO 80504-9200
Tel: 303-776-2337
E-mail: honey@nhb.org
http://www.honey.com

For information on the agricultural industry, contact
U.S. Department of Agriculture
1400 Independence Avenue, SW
Washington, DC 20250-0002
Tel: 202-720-2791
http://www.usda.gov

INTERVIEW

Howland Blackiston, the author of Beekeeping For Dummies *(For Dummies, 2009), has been a beekeeper since 1981. He has written many articles on beekeeping and has appeared on dozens of television shows and radio programs and in numerous magazines. Howland is also the founder of Bee-Commerce (http://www.bee-commerce.com), an Internet-based superstore that offers beekeeping supplies and equipment for the hobbyist beekeeper, and is past president of Connecticut's Back Yard Beekeepers Association, one of the nation's largest regional clubs for the hobbyist beekeeper. He spoke to the editors of* Careers in Focus: Agriculture *about his experiences as a beekeeper.*

Q. How did you become interested and involved in beekeeping?

A. My first introduction to life inside the honeybee hive occurred many years ago during a school assembly. My classmates and I were shown a wonderful movie about the secret inner workings of the beehive. The film mesmerized me. I'd never seen anything so remarkable and fascinating. How could a bug be so smart and industrious? I couldn't help being captivated by the bountiful honeybee. That brief childhood event planted a seed that blossomed into a treasured hobby some 20 years later.

Q. As a beekeeping hobbyist, what sorts of activities do you do?

A. As a beekeeper you continually discover new things about nature, bees, and their remarkable social behavior. Just about any school, nature center, garden club, or youth organization loves for you (as a beekeeper) to share your knowledge. Each year I make the rounds with my slide show and props, sharing the miracle of honeybees with my community. On many occasions my daughter's teacher and classmates visited the house for an on-site workshop. I opened the hive and gave each wide-eyed student a close-up look at bees at work. Spreading the word to others about the value these little creatures bring to all of us is great fun. You're planting a seed for our next generation of beekeepers. After all, a grade-school presentation on beekeeping is what aroused my interest in honeybees.

I maintain half a dozen hives on my property in Weston, Connecticut. Beekeeping isn't labor intensive. Sure, you'll spend a weekend putting together your new equipment. And beekeepers just love to spend every chance they can get visiting their bees. But frequent visits are optional. The actual time that you absolutely must spend with your bees is surprisingly modest. Other than your first year (when I urge new beekeepers to inspect the hive frequently to find out more about their bees), you need to make only five to six visits to your hives every year. Add to that the time that you spend harvesting honey, repairing equipment, and putting things away for the season, and you'll probably devote 19 to 28 hours a year to your hobby (more if you make a business out of it).

I pretty much work solo at this hobby, although my family and neighbors enthusiastically chip-in during honey harvest weekend. Their reward? Fresh, pure honey still warm from the hive.

Q. **To some people, beekeeping can seem like a dangerous venture. What sorts of safety precautions do you take? Do beekeepers often get stung?**

A. Perhaps the best-known part of the bee's anatomy is its stinger. Quite honestly, that was my biggest apprehension about taking up beekeeping. I don't think I've ever been stung by a honeybee, but I'd certainly felt the wrath of yellow jackets and hornets. I wanted no part of becoming a daily target for anything so unpleasant. I fretted about my fear for a long time, looking for reassurances from experienced beekeepers. They told me time and again that honeybees bred for beekeeping were docile and seldom inclined to sting. But lacking firsthand experience, I was doubtful. The advice turned out to be 100 percent correct. Honeybees are docile and gentle creatures. To my surprise (and delight), I made it through my entire first season without receiving a single sting. In the nearly 20 years that I've been keeping bees, not a single member of my family, not a single visitor to my home, and not a single neighbor has ever been stung by one of my honeybees.

If you run like a banshee every time you see an insect, I suspect that beekeeping will be an uphill challenge for you. But if you love animals, nature, and the outdoors, and if you're curious about how creatures communicate and contribute to our environment, you'll be captivated by honeybees. If you like the idea of "farming" on a small scale, or you're intrigued by the prospect of harvesting your own all-natural honey, you'll enjoy becoming a beekeeper.

Do I ever get stung? Sure. But usually not more than three or four times a year. In every case, the stings I take are a result of my own carelessness. I'm rushing, taking shortcuts, or am inattentive to their moods—all things that I shouldn't do. The secret to avoiding stings is your technique and demeanor. Here are some helpful tips for avoiding stings:

- Always wear a veil and use your smoker when visiting your hive.
- Inspect your bees during pleasant daytime weather. Try to use the hours between 10:00 A.M. and 5:00 P.M. That's when most of the bees are out working, and fewer bees are at home. Don't open up the hive at night, during bad weather, or if a thunderstorm is brewing.

- Don't rush. Take your time and move calmly. Sudden movements are a no-no.
- Get a good grip on frames. If you drop a frame of bees, you'll have a memorable story to tell.
- Never swat at bees. Become accustomed to them crawling on your hands and clothing. They're just exploring. Bees can be gently pushed aside if necessary.
- When woodenware is stuck together with propolis [a resinous, waxy material bees collect from the buds of trees], don't snap it apart with a loud "crack." The bees go on full alert when they feel sudden vibrations.
- Never leave sugar syrup or honey in open containers near the hive. Doing so can excite bees into a frenzy, and you may find yourself in the middle of it. It can also set off robbing—an unwelcome situation in which bees from other colonies attack your bees, robbing them of their honey.
- Keep yourself and bee clothing laundered. Bees don't like bad body odor. If you like to eat garlic, avoid indulging right before visiting your bees.
- Wear light-colored clothing. Bees don't seem to like dark colors.

Q. What are some of the benefits of beekeeping?

A. Why has mankind been so interested in beekeeping over the centuries? I'm sure that the first motivator was honey. After all, for many years and long before cane sugar, honey was the primary sweetener in use. I'm also sure that honey remains the principal draw for many backyard beekeepers. But the sweet reward is by no means the only reason folks are attracted to beekeeping. For a long time, the agricultural community has recognized the value of pollination by bees. Without the bees' help, many commercial crops would suffer serious consequences. Even backyard beekeepers witness dramatic improvements in their gardens' yields: more and larger fruits, flowers, and vegetables. A hive or two in the garden makes a big difference in your success as a gardener. The rewards of beekeeping extend beyond honey and pollination. Bees produce other products that can be harvested and put to good use, including beeswax, propolis, and royal jelly. Even the pollen they bring back to the hive can be harvested (it's rich in protein and makes a healthy food supplement in our own diets).

Although I can't point to any scientific studies to confirm it, I honestly believe that tending honeybees reduces stress. Working with my bees is so calming—almost magical. I am at one with nature, and whatever problems may have been on my mind tend to evaporate. There's something about being out there on a lovely warm day, the intense focus of exploring the wonders of the hive, and hearing that gentle hum of contented bees—it instantly puts me at ease, melting away whatever day-to-day stresses that I might find creeping into my life.

Any health food store proprietor can tell you the benefits of the bees' products. Honey, pollen, royal jelly, and propolis have been a part of healthful remedies for centuries. Honey and propolis have significant antibacterial qualities. Royal jelly is loaded with B vitamins and is widely used overseas as a dietary and fertility stimulant. Pollen is high in protein and can be used as a homeopathic remedy for seasonal pollen allergies.

Q. How can someone who is interested in beekeeping become involved in the field?

A. The first question to ask is, "When should I start on this adventure?" Winter is an ideal time to start beekeeping. Winter is a good time to order and assemble the equipment that you'll need and to reserve a package of bees for early spring delivery. Use the winter months to read up on bees and beekeeping and become familiar with your equipment. I unmodestly suggest my own book, *Beekeeping For Dummies*. Be sure to join a bee club and attend their meetings. That's a great way to learn more about beekeeping and meet new friends.

Q. What are the most important qualities of successful beekeepers?

A. The secret to being successful is best explained by understanding a subtle difference in terms . . . *having* bees is not the same as *keeping* bees. Bee "havers" are passive about their hive(s). Sure they "have" beehives on their property, but they do little or nothing to manage and tend to their "girls." They pretty much hold their breath and gamble that all goes well. In contrast, bee "keepers" love tending to their bees. They diligently monitor the bees' needs, provide space as the colony grows, and ensure that the colony is healthy and well fed. They systematically follow a simple regimen throughout the season to optimize the colony's welfare. Bee havers are not beekeepers. Therein [is] the secret to success.

Commodities Brokers

OVERVIEW

Commodities brokers, also known as *futures commission merchants*, act as agents in carrying out purchases and sales of commodities for customers or traders. Commodities are primary goods that are either raw or partially refined. Examples include goods produced by farmers, such as corn, wheat, or cattle, or mined from the earth, such as gold, copper, or silver. Brokers, who may work at a brokerage house, on the floor of a commodities exchange, or independently, are paid a fee or commission for acting as the middleman to conduct and complete the trade. Approximately 317,200 securities, commodities, and financial services sales agents (a group including commodities brokers) are employed in the United States.

HISTORY

In medieval Europe, business was transacted at local market fairs, and commodities, primarily agricultural, were traded at scheduled times and places. As market fairs grew, "fair letters" were set up as a currency representing a future cash settlement for a transaction. With these letters, merchants could travel from one fair to another. This was the precursor to the Japanese system, in which landowners used "certificates of receipt" for their rice crops. As the certificates made their way into the economy, the Dojima Rice Market was established and became the first place where traders bought and sold contracts for the future delivery of rice.

"Forward contracts" entered the U.S. marketplace in the early 19th century. Farmers, swept up in the boom of industrial growth, transportation, and commerce, began to arrange for the future sale of their crops. Traders entered the market along with the development of these contracts. However, there were no regulations to oversee that the commodity was actually delivered or that it was of an acceptable quality. Furthermore, each transaction was an individual business deal because the terms of each contract were variable. To address these issues, the Chicago Board of Trade was formed in 1848, and by 1865 it had set up standards and rules for trading "to arrive" contracts, now known as commodity futures contracts. In 2007, the Chicago Board of Trade merged with the Chicago Mercantile Exchange to become the CME Group.

THE JOB

A futures contract is an agreement to deliver a particular commodity, such as wheat, pork bellies, or coffee, at a specific date, time, and place. For example, a farmer might sell his oats before they are sowed (known as hedging) because he cannot predict what kind of price he will be able to demand later on. If the weather is favorable and crops are good, he will have competition, which will drive prices down. If there is a flood or drought, oats will be scarce, driving the price up. He wants to ensure a fair price for his product to protect his business and limit his risk, since he cannot predict what will happen.

On the other side of the equation is the user of the oats, perhaps a cereal manufacturer, who purchases these contracts for a delivery of oats at some future date. Producers and users do not correspond to a one-to-one ratio, and the broker is a middleman who does the buying and selling of contracts between the two groups. Brokers may place orders to buy or sell contracts for themselves, for individual clients, or for companies, all of who hope to make a profit by correctly anticipating the direction of a commodity's price. Brokers are licensed to represent clients, and brokers' first responsibility is to take care of their clients' orders before doing trading for themselves. *Traders* also buy and sell contracts for themselves. Unlike brokers, however, they are not licensed (and thus not allowed) to do this work for clients.

When placing a trade for others, brokers are paid a fee or a commission for acting as the agent in making the sale. There are two broad categories of brokers, though they are becoming less distinct. *Full service brokers* provide considerable research to clients, offer price quotes, give trading advice, and assist the customer in making trading decisions. *Discount brokers* simply fill the orders as directed by clients. Some brokers offer intermediate levels of optional services on a sliding scale of commission, such as market research and strategic advice.

In general, brokers are responsible for taking and carrying out all commodity orders and being available on call to do so; reporting back to the client upon fulfilling the order request; keeping the client abreast of breaking news; maintaining account balances and other financial data; and obtaining market information when needed and informing the client about important changes in the marketplace.

Brokers can work on the floor of a commodity futures exchange—the place where contracts are bought and sold—for a brokerage house, or independently. The exchange has a trading floor where brokers transact their business in the trading pit. There are 10 domestic exchanges, with the main ones in Chicago, Kansas City, New York, and Minneapolis. To be allowed to work on the floor, a broker must have a membership (also known as a "seat") in the exchange or must be employed by a company with a seat in the exchange, which is a private organization. Memberships are limited to a specific number, and seats may be rented or purchased. Although seat prices vary due to factors such as the health of the overall economy and the type of seat being purchased, they are all extremely expensive. Seat prices can range from tens of thousands of dollars to hundreds of thousands of dollars (full seats have been known to sell for $700,000 and more). Naturally, this expense alone limits the number of individuals who can become members. In addition to being able to afford a seat, candidates for membership to any exchange must undergo thorough investigations of their credit standings, financial backgrounds, characters, and understanding of trading.

Most brokers do not have seats but work for brokerage houses that deal in futures. Examples of these houses include Merrill Lynch or Morgan Stanley, which deal in stocks, bonds, commodities, and other investments, and smaller houses, such as R.J. O'Brien and Associates LLC, that handle only commodities.

Companies can also have a seat on the exchange, and they have their own *floor brokers* in the pit to carry out trades for the brokerage house. Brokers in the company take orders from the public for buying or selling a contract and promptly pass it on to the floor broker in the pit of the exchange. *Specialists* or *market makers* also work on the exchange floor. According to the U.S. Department of Labor (DOL), "There is generally one for each security or commodity being traded. They facilitate the trading process by quoting prices and by buying or selling shares when there are too many or too few available." Brokers also have the choice of running their own business. Known as *introducing brokers,* they handle their own clients and trades and use brokerage houses to place their orders. Introducing brokers earn a fee by soliciting business trades, but they don't directly handle the customer's funds.

REQUIREMENTS

High School

A bachelor's degree in business, finance, accounting, or economics is strongly recommended for brokers. Commodities brokers need to have a wide range of knowledge, covering such areas as economics, world politics, and sometimes even the weather. To begin to develop this broad base of knowledge, start in high school by taking history, math, science, and business classes. Since commodities brokers are constantly working with people to make a sale, take English classes to enhance your communication skills. In addition to this course work, you might also consider getting a part-time job working in a sales position. Such a job will also give you the chance to hone your communication and sales skills.

Postsecondary Training

The vast majority of brokers have a college degree. While there is no "commodities broker major," you can improve your chances of obtaining a job in this field by studying economics, finance, accounting, or business administration while in college. Keep in mind that you should continue to develop your understanding of politics and technologies, so government and computer classes will also be useful. Some commodities brokers also go on to earn master's degrees in business administration. Brokers also receive intensive on-the-job training from their employers after they are hired.

Brokerage firms look for employees who have sales ability, strong communication skills, and self-confidence. Commodities is often a second career for many people who have demonstrated these qualities in other positions.

Certification or Licensing

To become a commodities broker, it is necessary to pass the National Commodities Futures Examination (the Series 3 exam) to become eligible to satisfy the registration requirements of federal, state, and industry regulatory agencies. The test covers market and trading knowledge as well as rules and regulations and is composed of true/false and multiple-choice questions. Registration for the exam is through the Financial Industry Regulatory Authority (http://www.finra.org). Preparation materials are available through a number of sources, such as the Institute for Financial Markets (http://www.

theifm.org). Brokers must also register with the National Futures Association (http://www.nfa.futures.org).

Other Requirements

To be a successful broker, you must possess a combination of research and money management skills. You need to be attentive to detail and have a knack for analyzing data. Strong communication and sales skills are important as well, as brokers make money by convincing people to let them place their trades. An interest in and awareness of the world around you will also be a contributing factor to your success in this field, as commodities are influenced by everything from political decisions and international news to social and fashion trends.

You must also be emotionally stable to work in such a volatile environment. You need to be persistent, aggressive, and comfortable taking risks and dealing with failure. Strong, consistent, and independent judgment is also key. You must be a disciplined hard worker, able to comb through reams of market reports and charts to gain a thorough understanding of a particular commodity and the mechanics of the marketplace. You also need to be outspoken and assertive and able to yell out prices loudly and energetically on the trading floor (in settings where the open outcry format is still used) and to command attention.

EXPLORING

Students interested in commodities trading should visit one of the futures exchanges. All of them offer public tours, and you'll get to see up close just how the markets work and the roles of the players involved. All the exchanges offer educational programs and publications, and most have a Web site (see For More Information at the end of this article). The CME Group publishes *An Introduction to Futures and Options,* the full text of which is available at http://www.cmegroup.com/files/intro_fut_opt.pdf. There are hundreds of industry newsletters and magazines available (such *as Futures Magazine,* available at http://www.futuresmag.com), and many offer free samples of publications or products. Read what trading advisers have to say and how they say it. Learn their lingo and gain an understanding of the marketplace. If you have any contacts in the industry, arrange to spend a day with a broker. Watch him or her at work, and you'll learn how orders are entered, processed, and reported.

Do your own research. Adopt a commodity, chart its prices, test some of your own ideas, and analyze the marketplace. There are also a variety of inexpensive software programs, as well as Web sites, that simulate trading.

Finally, consider a job as a *runner* during the summer before your freshman year in college. Runners transport the order, or "paper," from the phone clerk to the broker in the pit and relay information to and from members on the floor. This is the single best way to get hands-on experience in the industry.

EMPLOYERS

Approximately 317,200 securities, commodities, and financial services sales agents (a group including commodities brokers) are employed in the United States. Commodities brokers work on the floor of a commodity futures exchange, for brokerage houses, or independently.

STARTING OUT

College graduates can start working with a brokerage house as an associate and begin handling stocks. After several years they can take the certification exam and move into futures. Another option is to start as support staff, either at the exchange or the brokerage house. Sales personnel try to get customers to open accounts, and account executives develop and service customers for the brokerage firm. At the exchange, *phone clerks* receive incoming orders and communicate the information to the runners. Working in the back as an accountant, money manager, or member of the research staff is also another route. College career services offices may be able to assist graduates in finding jobs with brokerage houses. Applications may also be made directly to brokerage houses.

Many successful brokers and traders began their careers as runners, and each exchange has its own training program. Though the pay is low, runners learn the business very quickly with hands-on experience not available in an academic classroom. Contact one of the commodities exchanges for information on becoming a runner.

ADVANCEMENT

A broker who simply executes trades can advance to become a full-service broker. Through research and analysis and the accumulation of experience and knowledge about the industry, a broker can advance from an order filler and become a commodity trading adviser. A broker can also become a money manager and make all trading decisions for clients.

Within the exchange, a broker can become a *floor manager,* over-seeing the processes of order taking and information exchange. To make more money, a broker can also begin to place his or her own trades for his or her own private account, though the broker's first responsibility is to the customers.

EARNINGS

This is an entrepreneurial business. A broker's commission is based on the number of clients he or she recruits, the amount of money they invest, and the profit they make. The sky's the limit. In recent years, the most successful broker made $25 million. A typical salary for a newly hired employee in a brokerage might average $1,500 per month plus a 30 percent commission on sales. Smaller firms are likely to pay a smaller commission. The DOL reports that the median annual earnings for securities, commodities, and financial services sales representatives (a group including commodities brokers) were $66,930 in 2009. The lowest paid 10 percent earned less than $29,980; the highest paid 25 percent earned more than $118,640 annually.

Benefits vary but are usually very good at large employers. For example, those working at one of the world's leading futures exchanges enjoy benefits such as vacation and sick days; medical, life, and disability insurance; and flextime during summer months. Full tuition reimbursement may also be available, as well as a company-matched savings plan, a tax-deferred savings plan, and a pension program.

WORK ENVIRONMENT

A growing number of exchanges now use electronic systems to auto-mate trades, and many use them exclusively. At exchanges that still use the "open outcry" system, the trading floor is noisy and chaotic. Every broker must be an auctioneer, yelling out his own price bids for purchases and sales. The highest bid wins and silences all the others. When a broker's primal scream is not heard, bids and offers can also be communicated with hand signals.

Brokers stand for most of the day, often in the same place, so that traders interested in their commodity can locate them easily. Each broker wears a distinctly colored jacket with a prominent identification badge. The letter on the badge identifies the broker and appears on the paperwork relating to the trade. Members of the exchange and employees of member firms wear red jackets. Some brokers and traders also have uniquely patterned jackets to further increase their visibility in the pit.

Brokers and traders do not have a nine-to-five job. While commodities trading on the exchange generally takes place from 9:00 A.M. to 1:00 P.M., international trading runs from 2:45 P.M. to 6:50 A.M.

In the rough and tumble world of the futures exchange, emotions run high as people often win or lose six- or seven-figure amounts within hours. Tension is fierce, the pace is frantic, and angry, verbal, and sometimes physical exchanges are not uncommon.

OUTLOOK

The DOL predicts that employment for securities, commodities, and financial services sales agents will grow about as fast as the average for all careers through 2018. Employment is expected to grow by 9 percent during this time span. The global financial crisis and the recession in the United States have caused the financial industry to contract, which has reduced the number of jobs for commodities brokers. Some growth will occur as a result of the growing number and increasing complexity of investment options and the new commodities available for investment due to the increasingly globalized marketplace. Additionally, as people and companies become more interested in and sophisticated about investing, they are entering futures markets and need the services provided by brokers. Baby boomers are reaching retirement age, and many are looking to invest in markets as a way of saving for their futures; additionally, many women in the workforce and higher household incomes means more investment.

New computer and information technology is rapidly influencing and advancing the industry. Many systems have unique features designed specifically to meet customers' needs. New technology, such as electronic order entry, links to overseas exchanges, and night trading, is rapidly evolving, offering brokers new ways to manage risk and provide price information.

Because many people are attracted to this work by the possibility of earning large incomes, competition for jobs is particularly keen. However, job turnover is also fairly high due to the stress of the work and the fact that many beginning brokers are not able to establish a large enough clientele to be profitable. Small brokerage firms will offer the best opportunities for those just starting out in this work.

FOR MORE INFORMATION

This center provides information on workshops, home study courses, educational materials, and publications for futures and securities professionals.

Center for Futures Education
PO Box 309
Grove City, PA 16127-0309
Tel: 724-458-5860
E-mail: info@thectr.com
http://www.thectr.com

For a general overview of options, visit the CBOE Web site.

Chicago Board Options Exchange (CBOE)
400 South LaSalle Street
Chicago, IL 60605-1023
Tel: 877-THE-CBOE
http://www.cboe.com

The CME Group was formed in 2007 as a result of a merger between the Chicago Mercantile Exchange and the Chicago Board of Trade. Visit its Web site for a wide variety of educational programs and materials, and general information on commodities careers.

CME Group
Tel: 800-331-3332
E-mail: info@cmegroup.com
http://www.cmegroup.com

For information on the commodities futures industry, contact

Commodity Futures Trading Commission
Three Lafayette Centre
1155 21st Street, NW
Washington DC 20581-0001
Tel: 202-418-5000
http://www.cftc.gov

For more information on the National Commodities Futures Examination, contact

Financial Industry Regulatory Authority
1735 K Street, NW
Washington, DC 20006-1500
Tel: 301-590-6500
http://www.finra.org

For information on membership, training, and registration, contact
National Futures Association
120 Broadway, #1125
New York, NY 10271-1196
Tel: 212-608-8660
E-mail: information@nfa.futures.org
http://www.nfa.futures.org

Visit the Web sites or contact the following exchanges for general background information about the field:
IntercontinentalExchange
https://www.theice.com

Minneapolis Grain Exchange
http://www.mgex.com

For information on the agricultural industry, contact
U.S. Department of Agriculture
1400 Independence Avenue, SW
Washington, DC 20250-0002
Tel: 202-720-2791
http://www.usda.gov

Farm Equipment Mechanics

OVERVIEW

Farm equipment mechanics maintain, adjust, repair, and overhaul equipment and vehicles used in planting, cultivating, harvesting, moving, processing, and storing plant and animal farm products. Among the specialized machines with which they work are tractors, harvesters, combines, pumps, tilling equipment, silo fillers, hay balers, and sprinkler irrigation systems. They work for farm equipment repair shops, farm equipment dealerships, and on large farms that have their own shops. Approximately 31,200 farm equipment mechanics work in the United States.

HISTORY

The purpose of the mechanical devices used in farming has always been to increase production and decrease the need for human labor. In prehistoric times, people used simple wood and stone implements to help turn soil, plant seeds, and harvest crops more efficiently than they could with their bare hands. With the introduction of metal tools and the domestication of animals that could pull plows and vehicles, people were able to produce much more. Until the 19th century, farmers around the globe relied on human labor, animal power, and relatively simple equipment to accomplish all the tasks involved in agriculture.

Modern mechanized agriculture was developed in the 1800s. Initially, steam power was used for farm equipment. In the early part of the 20th century, gasoline-powered engines appeared. Shortly after, diesel engines were introduced to power various kinds of farm machinery. The use of motor-driven machines on farms had far-reaching effects. Machines improved agricultural productivity while lessening the need for human labor. As a result of increased use of farm machinery, the number of people working on farms has steadily decreased in many countries of the world.

In recent decades, farm machines have become large and complex, using electronic, computerized, and hydraulic systems. Agriculture is now a business operation that requires extremely expensive equipment capable of doing specialized tasks quickly and efficiently. Farmers cannot afford for their equipment to break down. They are now almost completely reliant on the dealers who sell them their equipment to be their source for the emergency repairs and routine maintenance services that keep the machines functioning well. Farm equipment mechanics are the skilled specialists who carry out these tasks, usually as employees of equipment dealers or of independent repair shops.

THE JOB

The success of today's large-scale farming operations depends on the reliability of many complex machines. It is the farm equipment mechanic's responsibility to keep the machines in good working order and to repair or to overhaul them when they break down.

When farm equipment is not working properly, mechanics begin by diagnosing the problem. Using intricate testing devices, they are

Learn More About It

Berry, Wendell. *Bringing It to the Table: On Farming and Food.* Berkeley, Calif.: Counterpoint, 2009.

Casper, Julie Kerr. *Agriculture: The Food We Grow and Animals We Raise.* New York: Chelsea House Publications, 2007.

Conkin, Paul Keith. *A Revolution Down on the Farm: The Transformation of American Agriculture Since 1929.* Lexington, Ky.: University Press of Kentucky, 2009.

Fried, Katrina, and Paul Mobley. *American Farmer: The Heart of Our Country.* New York: Welcome Books, 2008.

Hamilton, Lisa M. *Deeply Rooted: Unconventional Farmers in the Age of Agribusiness.* Berkeley, Calif.: Counterpoint, 2010.

Whitman, Ann, Suzanne DeJohn, and The National Gardening Association. 2d ed. *Organic Gardening For Dummies.* Hoboken, N.J.: For Dummies, 2009.

able to identify what is wrong. A compression tester, for example, can determine whether cylinder valves leak or piston rings are worn, and a dynamometer can measure engine performance. The mechanic will also examine the machine, observing and listening to it in operation and looking for clues such as leaks, loose parts, and irregular steering, braking, and gear shifting. It may be necessary to dismantle whole systems in the machine to diagnose and correct malfunctions.

When the problem is located, the broken, worn-out, or faulty components are repaired or replaced, depending on the extent of their defect. The machine or piece of equipment is reassembled, adjusted, lubricated, and tested to be sure it is again operating at its full capacity.

Farm equipment mechanics use many tools in their work. Besides hand tools such as wrenches, pliers, and screwdrivers, and precision instruments such as micrometers and torque wrenches, they may use welding equipment, power grinders and saws, and other power tools. In addition, they do major repairs using machine tools such as drill presses, lathes, and milling and woodworking machines.

As farm equipment becomes more complex, mechanics are increasingly expected to have strong backgrounds in electronics. For instance, newer tractors have large, electronically controlled engines and air-conditioned cabs, as well as transmissions with many speeds.

Much of the time, farmers can bring their equipment into a shop, where mechanics have all the necessary tools available. But during planting or harvesting seasons, when timing may be critical for the farmers, mechanics are expected to travel to farms for emergency repairs in order to get the equipment up and running with little delay.

Farmers usually bring movable equipment into a repair shop on a regular basis for preventive maintenance services such as adjusting and cleaning parts and tuning engines. Routine servicing not only ensures less emergency repairs for the mechanics, but it also assures farmers that the equipment will be ready when it is needed. Shops in the rural outskirts of metropolitan areas often handle maintenance and repairs on a variety of lawn and garden equipment, especially lawn mowers.

If a mechanic works in a large shop, he or she may specialize in specific types of repairs. For example, a mechanic may overhaul gasoline or diesel engines, repair clutches and transmissions, or concentrate on the air-conditioning units in the cabs of combines and large tractors. Some mechanics, called *farm machinery set-up mechanics,* uncrate, assemble, adjust, and often deliver machinery to farm locations. Mechanics also do body work on tractors and other machines, repairing damaged sheet-metal body parts.

Some mechanics may work exclusively on certain types of equipment, such as hay balers or harvesters. Other mechanics work on equipment that is installed on the farms. For example, *sprinkler-irrigation equipment mechanics* install and maintain self-propelled circle-irrigation systems, which are like giant motorized lawn sprinklers. *Dairy equipment repairers* inspect and repair dairy machinery and equipment such as milking machines, cream separators, and churns.

Most farm equipment mechanics work in the service departments of equipment dealerships. Others are employed by independent repair shops. A smaller number work on large farms that have their own shops.

REQUIREMENTS

High School

Take technical/shop courses that will introduce you to machinery repair, electrical work, and welding. Mechanical drawing classes can also prepare you for the work. Computer courses will be valuable; computers are used increasingly in farm machinery, as well as in the administrative office of a machine repair and sales business. Science courses that include units in soil and agronomy will help you to understand the needs of the agriculture industry. As a member of the National FFA Organization (formerly the Future Farmers of America), you may be involved in special projects that include working with farm machinery.

Postsecondary Training

After graduating from high school, most farm equipment mechanics go on to complete a one- or two-year program in agricultural or farm mechanics at a vocational school or community college. If you cannot find such a program, study in diesel mechanics or appropriate experience through the military are also options. Topics that you will learn about include the maintenance and repair of diesel and gasoline engines, hydraulic systems, welding, and electronics. Your education does not stop there, however. After completing one of these programs you will be hired as a trainee or helper and continue to learn on the job, receiving training from experienced mechanics.

Some farm equipment mechanics learn their trade through apprenticeship programs. These programs combine three to four years of on-the-job training with classroom study related to farm equipment repair and maintenance. Apprentices are usually chosen from among shop helpers.

To stay up-to-date on technological changes that affect their work, mechanics and trainees may take special short-term courses conducted by equipment manufacturers. In these programs, which usually last a few days, company service representatives explain the design and function of new models of equipment and teach mechanics how to maintain and repair them. Some employers help broaden their mechanics' skills by sending them to local vocational schools for special intensive courses in subjects such as air-conditioning repair, hydraulics, or electronics.

Other Requirements

Farm machinery is usually large and heavy. Mechanics need the strength to lift heavy machine parts, such as transmissions. They also need manual dexterity to be able to handle tools and small components. Farm equipment mechanics are usually expected to supply their own hand tools. After years of accumulating favorite tools, experienced mechanics may have collections that represent an investment of thousands of dollars. Employers generally provide all the large power tools and test equipment needed in the shop. Other important traits include the ability to understand technical manuals, strong computer skills, knowledge of computer technology, and a willingness to continue to learn throughout one's career.

EXPLORING

Many people who go into farm equipment work have grown up with mechanical repair—they have experimented with lawn mowers, old cars, and other machinery, and they have used a lot of farm equipment. If you do not live on a farm, you may be able to find part-time or summer work on a farm. You can also get valuable mechanical experience working at a gasoline service station, automobile repair shop, or automotive supply house. Attending farm shows is a good way to learn about farm equipment and manufacturers. At shows, you may have the opportunity to talk to equipment manufacturers' representatives and learn more about new developments in the industry. In addition, consider joining a chapter of the National FFA Organization. This organization is open to students aged 12 to 21 enrolled in agricultural programs and offers a wide variety of activities, including career-development programs.

EMPLOYERS

Approximately 31,200 farm equipment mechanics are employed in the United States. Farm equipment mechanics work in all parts of the country, but there are more job opportunities in the "farm belt"—

the Midwestern states, as well as in California, Texas, and Florida. Work is available with independent repair and service businesses, large farm equipment sales companies, and large independent and commercial farms. Some mechanics are self-employed, running their own repair businesses in rural areas. Most independent repair shops employ fewer than five mechanics, while in dealers' service departments there may be 10 or more mechanics on the payroll.

STARTING OUT

Many people who become trainees in this field have prior experience in related occupations. They may have worked as farmers, farm laborers, heavy-equipment mechanics, automobile mechanics, or air-conditioning mechanics. Although people with this kind of related experience are likely to begin as helpers, their training period may be considerably shorter than the training for beginners with no such experience.

When looking for work, you should apply directly to local farm equipment dealers or independent repair shops. Graduates of vocational schools can often get help finding jobs through their schools' career services office. State employment service offices are another source of job leads, as well as a source of information on any apprenticeships that are available in the region.

ADVANCEMENT

After they have gained some experience, farm equipment mechanics employed by equipment dealers may be promoted to such positions as shop supervisor, service manager, and eventually manager of the dealership. Some mechanics eventually decide to open their own repair shops (about 6 percent of all mechanics are self-employed). Others become service representatives for farm equipment manufacturers. Additional formal education, such as completion of a two-year associate's degree program in agricultural mechanics or a related field, may be required of service representatives.

EARNINGS

Farm equipment mechanics had median hourly earnings of $15.85 in 2009, according to the U.S. Department of Labor (DOL). This figure translates into a yearly income of approximately $32,970. In addition, the department reports that the lowest paid 10 percent of farm equipment mechanics earned less than $10.52 per hour ($21,880 per year), while the highest paid 10 percent earned $23.11 or more per hour ($48,070 or more per year). Exact earnings figures are difficult to determine because farm equipment mechanics do not generally work consistent 40-hour weeks throughout the year. During the busy planting and harvest seasons, for example, mechanics may work many hours of overtime, for which they are usually paid time-and-a-half rates. This overtime pay can substantially increase their weekly earnings. However, during the winter months some mechanics may work less or they may be temporarily laid off, reducing their total income.

Employee benefits may be rare when working for a small shop. A large commercial farm or sales company may offer health insurance plans and sick leave.

WORK ENVIRONMENT

Farm equipment mechanics generally work indoors on equipment that has been brought into the shop. Most modern shops are properly ventilated, heated, and lighted. Some older shops may be less comfortable. During harvest seasons, mechanics may have to leave the shop frequently and travel many miles to farms, where they perform emergency repairs outdoors in any kind of weather. They may often work six to seven days a week, 10 to 12 hours a day during this busy season. In the event of an emergency repair, a mechanic often works independently, with little supervision. Mechanics need to be self-reliant and able to solve problems under pressure. When a farm machine breaks down, the lost time can be very expensive for the farmer. A mechanic must be able to diagnose problems quickly and perform repairs without delay.

Grease, gasoline, rust, and dirt are part of the farm equipment mechanic's life. Although safety precautions have improved in recent years, mechanics are often at risk of injury when lifting heavy equipment and parts with jacks or hoists. Other hazards they must routinely guard against include burns from hot engines, cuts from sharp pieces of metal, and exposure to toxic farm chemicals. Following good safety practices can reduce the risks of injury to a minimum.

OUTLOOK

The DOL reports that employment of farm equipment mechanics will grow about as fast as the average for all occupations through 2018. Although modern farm equipment has become more efficient and dependable, the increasing complexity of machinery, the growing population (which requires more food), and the increasing use of farm equipment to make biofuels will create good opportunities for farm equipment mechanics. To be competitive in the job market, farm equipment mechanics should complete a formal college training program.

Advancements in technology have revolutionized farm equipment. Those working with farm equipment will have to have an understanding of computers, electronics, and highly sophisticated devices and, therefore, more specialized training.

FOR MORE INFORMATION

For AEM press releases, equipment sales statistics, agricultural reports, and other news of interest to farm mechanics, contact
Association of Equipment Manufacturers (AEM)
6737 West Washington Street, Suite 2400
Milwaukee, WI 53214-5647
Tel: 414-272-0943
E-mail: aem@aem.org
http://www.aem.org

At the FEMA Web site, you can learn about its publications, read industry news, and find out about upcoming farm shows.
Farm Equipment Manufacturers Association (FEMA)
1000 Executive Parkway, Suite 100
St. Louis, MO 63141-6369
Tel: 314-878-2304
http://www.farmequip.org

For information on student chapters and the many activities available, contact
National FFA Organization
PO Box 68960
6060 FFA Drive
Indianapolis, IN 46268-0960
Tel: 317-802-6060
https://www.ffa.org

For information on the agricultural industry, contact
U.S. Department of Agriculture
1400 Independence Avenue, SW
Washington, DC 20250-0002
Tel: 202-720-2791
http://www.usda.gov

Farmers

OVERVIEW

Farmers either own or lease land on which they raise crops, such as corn, wheat, tobacco, cotton, vegetables, or fruits; raise animals or poultry; or maintain herds of dairy cattle for the production of milk. Whereas some farmers may combine several of these activities, most specialize in one specific area. They are assisted by *farm laborers*—either hired workers or members of farm families—who perform various tasks.

As increasingly complex technology continues to impact the agricultural industry, farms are becoming larger. Most contemporary farms are thousands of acres in size and include massive animal and plant production operations. Subsistence farms, which produce only enough to support the farmer's family, are becoming increasingly rare. There are approximately 985,900 farmers and ranchers employed in the United States.

HISTORY

In colonial America, almost 95 percent of the population were farmers, planting such crops as corn, wheat, flax, and, further south, tobacco. Livestock including hogs, cattle, sheep, and goats were imported from Europe. Farmers raised hay to feed livestock and often just enough other crops to supply their families with a balanced diet throughout the year. Progress in science and technology in the 18th and 19th centuries allowed for societies to develop in different directions, and to build other industries, but over one-half of the world's population is still engaged in farming today.

In the early 20th century, farmers raised a variety of crops along with cattle, poultry, and dairy cows. Farm labor was handled by the farmers and their families. Farmers were very self-sufficient, living on their farms and maintaining their own equipment and storage. Between 1910 and 1960, when horsepower was replaced by mechanized equipment, about 90 million acres previously devoted to growing hay for the feeding of horses could be planted with other crops. Advances in farming techniques and production led to larger farms and more specialization by farmers. Farmers began to focus on growing one or two crops. About this time, more tenant farmers entered the business, renting land for cash or share of the crops.

Farmers doubled their output between 1950 and 1980, but there were fewer of them. In that time, the farm population decreased from 23 million to 6 million. After 1980, many farmers began supplementing their household income with off-farm jobs and businesses.

Today, some small-scale farmers are finding success by catering to niche markets such as organic foods and specialty crops. Others are even branching off into aquaculture—the commercial farming of fish.

THE JOB

There are probably as many different types of farmers as there are different types of plants and animals whose products are consumed by humans. In addition to *diversified crops farmers,* who grow different combinations of fruits, grains, and vegetables, and *general farmers,* who raise livestock as well as crops, there are *cash grain farmers,* who grow barley, corn, rice, soybeans, and wheat; *vegetable farmers; tree-fruit-and-nut crops farmers; field crops farmers,* who raise alfalfa, cotton, hops, peanuts, mint, sugarcane, and tobacco; *animal breeders; fur farmers; livestock ranchers; dairy farmers; poultry farmers; beekeepers; reptile farmers; fish farmers;* and even *worm growers.*

In addition to the different types of crop farmers, there are two different types of farming management careers: the *farm operator* and the *farm manager.*

The farm operator either owns his or her own farm or leases land from other farms. Farm operators' responsibilities vary depending on the type of farm they run, but in general they are responsible for making managerial decisions. They determine the best time to seed, fertilize, cultivate, spray, and harvest. They keep extensive financial and inventory records of the farm operations, which are now done with the help of computer programs.

U.S. Farm Facts

Number of farms: 2,204,792

Total farmland: 922,095,840 acres

Most popular farm types: Cattle and calves, crops and hay, grains and oilseeds

Percent of farmland owned by farmers: 62 percent

Number of certified organic farms: 14,540

Top three organic products: Livestock, vegetables, field crops

Average farm size: 418 acres

Average age of farm Operators: 57.1 years

Percent of farmers who listed farming as their primary occupation: 45 percent

Top five agricultural commodities: Grains and oilseeds, milk, poultry and eggs, fruits and nuts, nursery and greenhouse

Source: 2007 Census of Agriculture, 2008 Organic Production Survey, U.S. Department of Agriculture

Farm operators perform tasks ranging from caring for livestock to erecting sheds. The size of the farm often determines what tasks the operators handle themselves. On very large farms, operators hire employees to perform tasks that operators on small farms would do themselves.

The farm manager has a wide range of duties. The owner of a large livestock farm may hire a farm manager to oversee a single activity, such as feeding the livestock. In other cases, a farm manager may oversee the entire operation of a small farm for an absentee owner. Farm management firms often employ highly skilled farm managers to manage specific operations on a small farm or to oversee tenant farm operations on several farms.

Whether farm operators or managers, the farmers' duties vary widely depending on what product they farm. A common type of farmer is the *crop farmer*. Following are a number of crops that a crop farmer might manage.

Corn farmers and *wheat farmers* begin the growing season by breaking up the soil with plows, then harrowing, pulverizing, and leveling it. Some of these tasks may be done after the harvest the previous year and others just before planting. Corn is usually planted around the middle of May with machines that place the corn seeds into dirt hills a few inches apart, making weed control easier. On the average, a crop is cultivated three times during a season. Corn is also used in the making of silage, a type of animal feed made by cutting the corn and allowing it to ferment in storage silos.

Wheat may be sown in the fall or spring, depending on the severity of the past winter and the variety of wheat being sown. Wheat is planted with a drill, close together, allowing greater cultivation and easier harvesting. The harvest for winter wheat occurs in early summer. Wheat farmers use machines called combines to gather and thresh the wheat in one operation. The wheat is then stored in large grain storage elevators, which are owned by private individuals, companies, or farming cooperatives.

Cotton and tobacco planting begins in March in the Southwest and somewhat later in the Southeast. Tobacco plants must be carefully protected from harsh weather conditions. The soil in which tobacco is grown must be thoroughly broken up, smoothed, and fertilized before planting, as tobacco is very hard on the soil.

The peanut crop can be managed like other types of farm crops. It is not especially sensitive to weather and disease, nor does it require the great care of tobacco and cotton.

Specialty crops such as fruits and vegetables are subject to seasonal variations, so the farmer usually relies heavily on hired seasonal labor. This type of farmer uses more specialized equipment than do general farmers.

The mechanization of farming has not eliminated all the problems of raising crops. Judgment and experience are always important in making decisions. The *hay farmer*, for example, must determine the time for mowing that will yield the best crop in terms of stem toughness and leaf loss. These decisions must be weighed against possible harsh weather conditions. To harvest hay, hay farmers use specialized equipment such as mowing machines and hay rakes that are usually drawn by tractors. The hay is pressed into bales by another machine for easier storage and then transported to storage facilities or to market.

Decisions about planting are just as crucial as those about harvesting. For example, potatoes need to be planted during a relatively short span of days in the spring. The fields must be tilled and ready

A farmer examines a crop of tomatoes at his farm. *(Peggy Greb, USDA, Agricultural Research Service)*

for planting, and the farmer must estimate weather conditions so the seedlings will not freeze from late winter weather.

The specialty crop farmer uses elaborate irrigation systems to water crops during seasons of inadequate rainfall. Often these systems are portable, as it is necessary to move the equipment from field to field.

Farms are strongly influenced by the weather, crop and animal diseases, fluctuations in prices of domestic and foreign farm products, and, in some cases, federal farm programs. Farmers must carefully plan the combination of crops they will grow so that if the price of one crop drops they will have sufficient income from another to make up for it. Since prices change from month to month, farmers who plan ahead may be able to store their crops or keep their livestock to take advantage of better prices later in the year.

Farmers who raise and breed animals for milk or meat are called livestock and cattle farmers. There are various types of farmers that fall into this category.

Livestock farmers generally buy calves from ranchers who breed and raise them. They feed and fatten young cattle and often raise their own corn and hay to lower feeding costs. They need to be familiar with cattle diseases and proper methods of feeding. They provide their cattle with fenced pasturage and adequate shelter from rough weather. Some livestock farmers specialize in breeding stock for sale to ranchers and dairy farmers. These specialists maintain and improve purebred animals of a particular breed. Bulls and cows are then sold to ranchers and dairy farmers who want to improve their herds.

Sheep ranchers raise sheep primarily for their wool. Large herds are maintained on rangeland in the western states. Since large areas of land are needed, the sheep rancher must usually buy grazing rights on government-owned lands.

Although *dairy farmers'* first concern is the production of high-grade milk, they also raise corn and grain to provide feed for their animals. Dairy farmers must be able to repair the many kinds of equipment essential to their business and know about diseases, sanitation, and methods of improving the quantity and quality of the milk.

Dairy animals must be milked twice every day, once in the morning and once at night. Records are kept of each cow's production of milk to ascertain which cows are profitable and which should be traded or sold for meat. After milking, when the cows are at pasture, the farmer cleans the stalls and barn by washing, sweeping, and sterilizing milking equipment with boiling water. This is extremely important because dairy cows easily contract diseases from unsanitary conditions, and this in turn may contaminate the milk. Dairy farmers must have their herds certified to be free of disease by the U.S. Department of Health and Human Services.

The great majority of *poultry farmers* do not hatch their own chicks but buy them from commercial hatcheries. The chicks are kept in brooder houses until they are seven or eight weeks old and are then transferred to open pens or shelters. After six months, the hens begin to lay eggs, and roosters are culled from the flock to be sold for meat.

The primary duty of poultry farmers is to keep their flocks healthy. They provide shelter from the chickens' natural enemies and from extreme weather conditions. The shelters are kept extremely clean, because diseases can spread through a flock rapidly. The poultry farmer selects the food that best allows each chicken to grow or produce to its greatest potential while at the same time keeping costs down.

Raising chickens to be sold as broilers or fryers requires equipment to house them until they are six to 13 weeks old. Farmers specializing in the production of eggs gather eggs at least twice a day and more often in very warm weather. The eggs then are stored in a cool place, inspected, graded, and packed for market. The poultry farmer who specializes in producing broilers is usually not an independent producer but is under contract with a backer, who is often the operator of a slaughterhouse or the manufacturer of poultry feeds.

Aquaculture farmers, also known as *aquaculturists, fish farmers, fish culturists,* and *mariculturists,* raise fish, shellfish, or other aquatic life (such as aquatic plants) under controlled conditions for profit and/or human consumption. (See Aquaculturists for more information.)

Beekeepers set up and manage beehives and harvest and sell the excess honey that bees don't use as their own food. The sale of honey is less profitable than the business of cultivating bees for lease to farmers to help pollinate their crops. (See Beekeepers for more information.)

Farmers and farm managers make a wide range of administrative decisions. In addition to their knowledge of crop production and animal science, they determine how to market the foods they produce. They keep an eye on the commodities markets to see which crops are most profitable. They take out loans to buy farm equipment or additional land for cultivation. They keep up with new methods of production and new markets. Farms today are large, complex businesses, complete with the requisite anxiety over cash flow, competition, markets, and production.

REQUIREMENTS

High School

Take classes in math, accounting, and business to prepare for the management responsibilities of running a farm. To further assist you in management and the use of farming-related technology, take computer classes. Chemistry, biology, and earth science classes can help you understand the various processes of crop production. Technical and shop courses will help you to better understand agricultural machinery. With county extension courses, you can keep abreast of developments in farm technology.

Postsecondary Training

Although there are no specific educational requirements for this field, every successful farmer, whether working with crops or animals, must know the principles of soil preparation and cultivation, disease control, and machinery maintenance, as well as a mastery of business practices and bookkeeping. Farmers must know their crops well enough to be able to choose the proper seeds for their particular soil and climate. They also need experience in evaluating crop growth and weather cycles. Livestock and dairy farmers should enjoy working with animals and have some background in animal science, breeding, and care.

The state land-grant universities across the country (with at least one in every state) were established to encourage agricultural research and to educate young people in the latest advancements in farming. They offer agricultural programs that award bachelor's degrees as well as shorter programs in specific areas. Many students earn a degree in business with a concentration in agriculture, agricultural economics and business, animal science, agronomy, crop and fruit science, dairy science, farm management, or horticulture. Some universities offer advanced studies in horticulture, animal science, agronomy, and agricultural economics. Most students in agricultural colleges are also required to take courses in farm management, business, finance, and economics. Two-year colleges often have programs leading to associate's degrees in agriculture. It is highly recommended that farm managers and farmers earn at least an associate's degree in agriculture or a related subject (or business with a concentration in agriculture) in order to stay up-to-date with technological advancements and changes in farming practices.

A bachelor's degree in aquaculture or fish and wildlife biology are the primary paths into the field of aquaculture. A minor in business or accounting may also be valuable to a prospective aquaculturist. Course work focuses on hydrology, fisheries biology, fish culture, and hatchery management and maintenance.

Many people become beekeepers by receiving informal on-the-job training working with an experienced beekeeper. Community or junior colleges that offer agriculture classes may also provide another avenue for learning about honey production and bee care. Finally, some states may offer apprenticeship programs in beekeeping.

Certification or Licensing
The American Society of Farm Managers and Rural Appraisers offers farm operators voluntary certification as an accredited farm manager. Certification requires five years' experience working on a farm, an academic background—a bachelor's or preferably a master's degree in a branch of agricultural science—and completion of courses covering the business, financial, and legal aspects of farm management.

Other Requirements
You'll need to keep up-to-date on new farming methods throughout the world. You must be flexible and innovative enough to adapt to new technologies that will produce crops or raise livestock more efficiently. You should also have good mechanical aptitude and be able to work with a wide variety of tools and machinery. Other important traits include a good work ethic, determination, organizational skills, and business acumen.

EXPLORING
Most people who become farmers have grown up on farms; if your family doesn't own a farm, there are opportunities for part-time work as a hired hand, especially during seasonal operations. If you live in an agricultural community, you should be able to find work as a detasseler in the summer time. Although the work is hot and strenuous, it will quickly familiarize you with aspects of crop production and the hard work it takes to operate a farm.

In addition, organizations such as the National 4-H Council (http://4-h.org) and the National FFA Organization (https://www.ffa.org) offer good opportunities for learning about, visiting, and participating in farming activities. Agricultural colleges often have their own farms where students can gain actual experience in farm operations in addition to classroom work.

If you are between the ages of five and 22, you might also want to join the National Junior Horticulture Association, which offers horticulture-related projects, contests, and other activities, as well as career information. Visit http://www.njha.org for more information. In addition, consider joining a chapter of the National FFA Organization. This organization is open to students aged 12 to 21 enrolled in agricultural programs and offers a wide variety of activities, including career-development programs.

EMPLOYERS

Approximately 985,900 farmers and ranchers are employed in the United States. Nearly 80 percent of farmers are self-employed, working on land they've inherited, purchased, or leased. Those who don't own land, but who have farming experience, may find work on large commercial farms or with agricultural supply companies as consultants or managers. Farmers with seasonal crops may work for agriculture-related businesses during the off-season or may work temporarily as farm hands for livestock farms and ranches. They may also own other businesses, such as those that specialize in farm equipment sales and service.

The states of Texas, Missouri, Iowa, Oklahoma, and Kentucky have the largest number of farms. California, Texas, Iowa, Nebraska, and Minnesota are the leading agricultural states in terms of economic output.

STARTING OUT

It is becoming increasingly difficult for a person to purchase land for farming. The capital investment in a farm today is so great that it is almost impossible for anyone to start from scratch. However, those who lack a family connection to farming or who do not have enough money to start their own farm can lease land from other farmers. Money for leasing land and equipment may be available from local banks or the U.S. Department of Agriculture's (USDA) Farm Service Agency.

Because the capital outlay is so high, many wheat, corn, and specialty crop farmers often start as *tenant farmers,* renting land and equipment. They may also share the cash profits with the owner of the land. In this way, these tenants hope to gain both the experience and cash to purchase and manage their own farms.

Livestock farmers generally start by renting property and sometimes animals on a share-of-the-profits basis with the owner. Government lands can be rented for pasture as well. Later, when the livestock farmer wants to own property, it is possible to borrow based on the estimated value of the leased land, buildings, and animals. Dairy farmers can begin in much the same way. However, loans are becoming more difficult to obtain. After several years of lenient loan policies, financial institutions in farm regions have tightened their requirements.

ADVANCEMENT

Farmers advance by buying their own farms or additional acreage to increase production and income. With a farm's success, a farmer can also invest in better equipment and technology and can hire managers and workers to attend to much of the farm's operation. This is true for crop, livestock, dairy, or poultry farmers. In farming, as in other fields, a person's success depends greatly on education, motivation, and keeping up with the latest developments.

EARNINGS

Farmers' incomes vary greatly from year to year, since the prices of farm products fluctuate according to weather conditions and the amount and quality of what all farmers were able to produce. A farm that shows a large profit one year may show a loss for the following year. Most farmers, especially those running small farms, earn incomes from nonfarm activities that are several times larger than their farm incomes. Farm incomes also vary greatly depending on the size and type of farm. In general, large farms generate more income than small farms. Exceptions include some specialty farms that produce low-volume—but high-quality—horticultural and fruit products.

The Economic Research Service of the USDA reports that the average farm household income was $76,258 in 2009. This income, it is important to note, includes earnings from off-farm jobs, businesses, and other sources.

Farmers and ranchers earned a median annual salary of $32,350 in 2009, according to the U.S. Department of Labor (DOL). Salaries ranged from less than $18,900 to more than $91,710.

Farm managers who worked full-time had median annual earnings of $59,450 in 2009, according to the DOL. The lowest paid 10 percent of farm managers earned less than $31,680 a year, and the top-paid 10 percent of all farm managers earned $103,210 or more a year.

Farmers must provide their own benefits, such as health and life insurance and a savings and pension program. Farm managers and operators typically receive benefits from their employer.

WORK ENVIRONMENT

The farmer's daily life has its rewards and dangers. Machine-related injuries, exposure to the weather, and illnesses caused by allergies or animal-related diseases are just some of the hazards that farmers face on a regular basis. In addition, farms are often isolated, away from many conveniences and necessities, such as immediate medical attention.

Farming can be a difficult and frustrating career, but for many it is a satisfying way of life. The hours are long and the work is physically strenuous, but working outdoors and watching the fruits of one's labor grow before one's eyes can be very rewarding. The changing seasons bring variety to the day-to-day work. Farmers seldom work five eight-hour days a week. When harvesting time comes or the weather is right for planting or spraying, farmers work long hours to see that everything gets done. Even during the cold winter months they stay busy repairing machinery and buildings. Dairy farmers and other livestock farmers work seven days a week year round.

OUTLOOK

Employment of farmers and ranchers is expected to decline through 2018, according to the DOL. The department predicts that employment for farm and ranch managers will grow more slowly than the average for all careers (which, in DOL terminology, means that there will actually be some employment growth) during that same time span as owners of farm property seek managers to oversee land and agricultural workers. Every year can be different for farmers, as production, expansion, and markets are affected by weather, exports, and other factors. Land prices are expected to drop some, but so are the prices for grain, hogs, and cattle. Throughout the 20th century, the U.S. government actively aided farmers, but in recent years has attempted to step back from agricultural production. But the state of farming today calls for more government involvement. Some trends that farmers may follow in their efforts to increase income include more diversified crop production; for example, farmers may choose to plant high-oil or high-protein corn, which bring more money in the marketplace. But these new grains also require different methods of storage and marketing. Other farmers are focusing on growing specialty or organic crops or taking advantage of increasing demand for ethanol by planting more corn. In 2007, U.S. farmers planted nearly 93 million acres of corn—the largest corn crop in 63 years, according to the National Agricultural Statistics Service. Corn crops continued to remain high in the following years. Other crops that are used to make ethanol include wheat, potatoes, and sugar cane. As a result of this trend, fewer acres of other crops—such as soybeans and cotton—are being planted.

Employment for farmers who produce crops that are used in land-scaping, such as shrubs, trees, and turf, will be better than farmers who grow traditional crops.

Large corporate farms are fast replacing the small farmer, who is being forced out of the industry by the spiraling costs of feed, grain, chemicals, land, and equipment. The late 1970s and early 1980s were an especially hard time for farmers. Many small farmers were forced to give up farming; some lost farms that had been in their families for generations. Some small-scale farmers, however, have found opportunities in organic food production, farmers' markets, and similar market niches that require more direct personal contact with their customers.

Despite the great difficulty in becoming a farmer today, there are many agriculture-related careers that involve people with farm production, marketing, management, and agribusiness. Those with an interest in farming will likely have to pursue these alternative career paths.

FOR MORE INFORMATION

The American Beekeeping Federation acts on behalf of the bee-keeping industry on issues affecting the interests and the economic viability of the various sectors of the industry. The organization offers a free beginning beekeeping information packet and sponsors an essay contest in conjunction with 4-H. For more information, contact

American Beekeeping Federation
3525 Piedmont Road, Building 5, Suite 300
Atlanta, GA 30305-1578
Tel: 404-760-2875
E-mail: info@abfnet.org
http://www.abfnet.org

The AFBF Web site features legislative news, state farm bureau news, online brochures, and information on Farm Bureau Programs such as AFBF Young Farmers & Ranchers Program. This program, for those 18 to 35 years of age, offers educational conferences, net-working opportunities, and competitive events.

American Farm Bureau Federation (AFBF)
600 Maryland Avenue, SW, Suite 1000W
Washington, DC 20024-2520
Tel: 202-406-3600
http://www.fb.org

For information on certification, contact
American Society of Farm Managers and Rural Appraisers
950 South Cherry Street, Suite 508
Denver, CO 80246-2664
Tel: 303-758-3513
http://www.asfmra.org

To learn about farmer-owner cooperatives and how cooperative businesses operate, contact
National Council of Farmer Cooperatives
50 F Street, NW, Suite 900
Washington, DC 20001-1530
Tel: 202-626-8700
http://www.ncfc.org

For information on farm policies, homeland security issues, and other news relating to the agricultural industry, visit the USDA Web site.
U.S. Department of Agriculture (USDA)
1400 Independence Avenue, SW
Washington, DC 20250-0002
Tel: 202-720-2791
http://www.usda.gov

For information about aquaculture, contact
World Aquaculture Society
143 J. M. Parker Coliseum
Louisiana State University
Baton Rouge, LA 70803-0001
Tel: 225-578-3137
http://www.was.org

Farmers' Market Managers/Promoters

OVERVIEW

Farmers' market managers/promoters manage farmers' markets, ensuring that operations comply with laws and regulations. Their duties are diverse, ranging from enlisting farmers to participate in the market and promoting the market to consumers, to hiring and managing staff, scheduling events, and handling correspondence and record- and bookkeeping. They may work for one market or multiple markets within specific regions.

HISTORY

Farmers' markets provide opportunities for farmers and craftsmen to sell their products—fruits, vegetables, herbs, cheeses, meats, baked goods, etc.— directly to consumers. They date back to ancient times, when public markets were the few places in existence where residents could find the items they needed for daily living. Cities encouraged public markets as a way to bring local and regional producers to the city to increase their business, as well as a way to help residents get healthy food that was priced fairly. Public markets also provided employment opportunities, encouraged farming near the city, and, as a result, helped prevent people from moving away.

One early American public market was the city-owned High Street Market in Philadelphia. The market started with just a few stalls in the early 1800s, and by the 1850s had grown to a series of sheds stretching across many streets, with breaks only at the intersections. Market space was organized and

QUICK FACTS

School Subjects
Business
Earth science
English
Mathematics

Personal Skills
Communication/ideas
Leadership/management

Work Environment
Indoors and outdoors
Primarily multiple locations

Minimum Education Level
Some postsecondary training

Salary Range
$8,864 to $21,690 to
$60,400+

Certification or Licensing
None available

Outlook
About as fast as the average

DOT
N/A

GOE
N/A

NOC
N/A

O*NET-SOC
N/A

divided according to the types of products being sold, such as vegetables, herbs, roots, produce, meat, fish, and earthenware. High Street Market was torn down in 1859 to make way for the construction of large, market houses that were owned by private companies. This followed the movement away from municipally owned and operated farmers' markets of the previous decades and toward privatization of the business. Today most farmers' markets operate on public property, with sponsorship from such nongovernmental groups as farmers' associations, chambers of commerce, community organizations, or food cooperatives.

Farmers' markets are set up in various ways to fit in with their environment. Some use already existing structures, such as bridges and elevated highways, as cover. For others, where these types of structures are not available, stalls are built, and tarps and other materials are used for shelter. Many markets are open year-round, rain or shine, with limited days and hours of operation each week. They sell what is being grown that season.

Farmer's markets may be temporary setups (easy to assemble and break down), situated in open squares in cities, such as the Union Square Greenmarket in New York City. The Council on the Environment of New York City started this market, and others like it, in 1976, after years of city residents complaining bitterly about the "brown lettuce" and "hard tomatoes" that were being sold in supermarkets. The first greenmarket in New York City consisted of 12 farmers in an empty lot, and has grown since to become a large network of greenmarkets throughout the five boroughs.

Pike Place Market in Seattle, Washington, is an example of an older, well-established public market situated in a permanent structure. The origins of the nine-acre Pike Place Market are symbolic of the spirit that still drives many farmers' markets today. The price of onions had increased tenfold between 1906 and 1907, and citizens were outraged and were not going to take it any longer. Middlemen had been gouging prices for years and people were tired of being ripped off. Seattle City Councilman Thomas Reveille came up with the idea of a public street market, where farmers could sell directly to consumers, therefore eliminating the middleman. Pike Place Market "opened" on August 17, 1907, with eight farmers selling produce from their wagons at the corner of Pike Street and First Avenue. Approximately 10,000 shoppers showed up, and by 11:00 a.m., the wagons were sold out of produce. The Pike Market building opened at the end of 1907. Today, the market features 200 year-round commercial businesses; 190 craftspeople; and 120 farmers who rent table space by the day.

Consumer demand for locally grown, fresh food continues to grow, and more farmers' markets are starting up every year. Between 1994 and 2009, the number of farmers' markets operating in the United States increased from 1,755 to 5,274.

THE JOB

Farmers' market managers/promoters oversee markets in which farmers sell their products to consumers. Because farming is seasonal, more than two-thirds of all managers work for markets that are set up in temporary facilities. According to a 2006 survey conducted by the Agricultural Marketing Service of the U.S. Department of Agriculture (USDA), farmers' markets in 2005 averaged 48,857 square feet in size, which is about the size of a medium-sized retail grocery store. The smallest farmers' market was 20 square feet, and the largest was 3.4 million square feet.

As with most management positions in other industries, farmers' market managers are responsible for a variety of tasks. The vending stalls need to be filled with farmers, so managers work closely with farmers, meeting with them to promote the market, field their questions, and negotiate the terms for vending. They set up contracts, vending sites, and schedules. They also hire staff and volunteers, and manage and oversee their work. Another big part of the job is customer relations. Many management positions require previous experience in handling customers. This means not only addressing questions and concerns while on-site at the market, but responding to consumers' e-mails and phone calls when working in the office.

The Pacific Coast Farmers' Market Association describes the job requirements for a market manager as follows: making sure the market operates in compliance with state law, health regulations, and association rules and regulations; overseeing the set-up, operation, cleanliness, and shutdown of the market; collecting payment from farmers at the end of each market day; updating business logs and reports, and making bank deposits; setting up and running a market information booth to address customers' questions; and assisting in scheduling and hosting farmers' market events.

A farmers' market manager/promoter is also responsible for advertising and marketing the market to attract consumers. He or she may create the ads and flyers, or hire an artist or graphic designer to create promotions for newspapers and magazines, as well as a Web designer to work on the market's Web site. The manager/promoter also spreads word about the market by networking and building relationships with businesses located within the community where the farmers' market is located.

REQUIREMENTS

High School

If you are interested in this work, a well-rounded high school education should include course work in business, math, earth science, English, and computer science. Take classes in agriculture and ecology if your school offers them. Knowledge of another language can be beneficial in communicating with customers, employees, and farmers from other countries, so be sure to take foreign language classes as well.

Postsecondary Training

Some farmers' markets may require managers to have an undergraduate degree, while others may prefer prior work experience at a farmers' market. Course work in business, marketing, advertising, agriculture, social sciences, environmental studies, communications, and English are beneficial.

Other Requirements

Management positions, in general, require strong, clear communication skills. This is especially true for farmers' market managers. They deal with a wide range of people, from the general public to farmers and employees. Patience, flexibility, and diplomacy serve this type of work well. Knowledge of farming and farming products is also especially helpful. Familiarity with software programs, such as Microsoft Word, Excel, and Publisher are essential for administrative work. And fluency in another language, such as Spanish, may come in handy. Creative skills are useful in successfully advertising and promoting farmers' markets. Negotiation skills are also helpful in attracting and securing vendors for the market.

EXPLORING

The best way to learn more about the farmers' market management field is to talk to a manager directly. You can find a market near you by visiting the USDA's *National Directory of Farmers' Markets* (http://apps.ams.usda.gov/FarmersMarkets) and keying in your zip code. Most farmers' markets have their own Web sites, so be sure to browse through them and find the hours of operation. When you visit the market, be sure to talk with farmers and market employees. Ask them what their work entails, what's involved in participating in the farmers' market, and if the market manager is onsite and available to chat. Trade publications and books about the farmers' market business will give you further insight and understanding of the various facets of this type of work. The bi-monthly trade publication *Farmers' Markets Today* (http://www.farmersmarketstoday.com/fmt) provides useful information for farmers' market managers, vendors, and farmers. You can also find numerous books targeted at farmers' marketing by visiting the Books for Farmers' Markets Web site (http://www.farmersmarketonline.com/a/farmersmarketbooks.htm).

EMPLOYERS

As you may have guessed, farmers' market managers and promoters work for farmers' markets. They may work for a single-business operation, and therefore be located at just one site, or they may be responsible for several farmers' markets or more within one or more counties.

STARTING OUT

Volunteering or working part time at a farmers' market is the best way to see firsthand how a market operates and what managers deal with on a regular basis. Membership in a professional association for farmers' market managers also provides access to educational workshops, events and conferences, networking opportunities, and job listings. You can find such resources by visiting the Web site of the North American Farmers' Direct Marketing Association (http://www.nafdma.com), or by conducting an Internet search for a professional association in the state in which you live.

   You can also learn a great deal about farmers' markets and see if this work interests you by reading the University of California's Farmers' Market Management Series publications, which are published through the school's Small Farm Program. Titles include *Starting a New Farmers' Market*, *Management Skills for Marketers*, and *Growing Your Farmers' Market*. Visit http://www.sfc.ucdavis.edu/farmers_market for more information.

ADVANCEMENT

Moving up in the farmers' market management field depends on the managers' years of experience. Those who work for small, single-market operations can advance by covering more markets within several counties or regions. Other ways to advance include starting their own farmers' market and consulting with other markets about business and promotion. They might become educators, working for universities that have farmers' market programs. They might also work for nonprofit organizations or government agencies that focus on farming and farmers' markets.

EARNINGS

Salaries for farmers' market managers will vary depending upon the size of the market and the scope of the manager's job. Smaller-sized farmers' markets and those that are relatively young are more dependent upon outside funding than are larger, more established businesses. Farmers' markets that have been around for a long time are usually self-sufficient, able to continue operating based on vendors' fees alone. Newer businesses are usually funded by a combination of sources, including vendors' fees, city or county governments, and nonprofit organizations. Many farmers' markets also participate in government-funded nutrition programs as a way to help fund their businesses as well as to help people in need receive better and fresher food. Managers who work for smaller and newer markets tend to have lower salaries, as may be expected. Those who work for larger, older businesses will generally bring in higher annual incomes. Also, because the work is seasonal, managers may be paid on an hourly basis, and may have to seek alternate work when the season ends.

According to findings from a 2006 survey by the USDA Agricultural Marketing Service, the average annual salary for paid farmers' market managers in 2005 was $14,323, with the lowest salary at $8,864 in the Rocky Mountain region, and the highest salary at $21,912 in the Mid-Atlantic region.

The U.S. Department of Labor (DOL) does not cite salaries specific to farmers' market managers, but lists the annual income for supervisors or managers of retail sales workers in 2009 as ranging from $21,690 to $60,400 or more per year. Those who worked for grocery stores averaged $38,000 per year. Farmers' market managers who work in regions where the climate allows for more permanent, year-round marketing may have salaries within these ranges.

WORK ENVIRONMENT

Farmers' markets are usually outdoors in cities, suburbs, and countryside settings. Farmers' market managers/promoters will work at least 40-hour workweeks, which can include weekends. They work indoors in offices, as well as on-site at the markets and in various weather conditions. They may travel to different sites if they manage more than one market, so a valid driver's license and the ability and willingness to drive will be required.

OUTLOOK

Demand for farm-fresh food has been on the rise for more than a decade. To meet this demand, the farmers' market business is also growing, which is good news for farmers' market managers. According to the Agricultural Marketing Service of the USDA, there were 1,755 farmers' markets operating in the United States in 1994. In 2004 that number had more than doubled to 3,706. Since then, even more markets have opened and begun operations. In 2009, there were 5,274 farmers' markets.

While the DOL forecasts a moderate decline in employment opportunities for farmers overall through 2018, many small-scale farming businesses and those in related professions are finding success in specialty niches, such as organic food production as well as in farmers' markets that cater to urban and suburban customers. Farmers' market managers will, therefore, be needed to help build and maintain relationships with farmers and to get word out to consumers about the markets.

FOR MORE INFORMATION

Find farmers' market news, reports, and publications on the trust's Web site.
American Farmland Trust
1200 18th Street, NW, Suite 800
Washington, DC 20036-2524
Tel: 202-331-7300
E-mail: info@farmland.org
http://www.farmland.org

Learn more about agricultural policy and advocacy by visiting the FMC Web site.
Farmers Market Coalition (FMC)
PO Box 331
Cockeysville, MD 21030-0331
http://www.farmersmarketcoalition.org

To find out more about the Farmers' Market Managers Mentoring Program, contact
Farmers' Market Federation of New York
117 Highbridge Street, Suite U-3
Fayetteville, NY 13066-1951
Tel: 315-637-4690
E-mail: deggert@nyfarmersmarket.com
http://www.nyfarmersmarket.com

Visit this association's Web site for membership information and other resources.
North American Farmers' Direct Marketing Association
62 White Loaf Road
Southampton, MA 01073-9251
Tel: 413-529-0386
http://www.nafdma.com

Learn more about issues regarding food, farming, natural resources, and rural development by visiting
U.S. Department of Agriculture
Economic Research Service
1800 M Street, NW
Washington, DC 20036-5831
http://www.ers.usda.gov

Food Technologists

OVERVIEW

Food technologists, sometimes known as food scientists, study the physical, chemical, and biological composition of food. They develop methods for safely processing, preserving, and packaging food and search for ways to improve its flavor and nutritional value. They also conduct tests to ensure that products, from fresh produce to packaged meals, meet industry and government standards. Approximately 13,400 food technologists are employed in the United States.

HISTORY

One of the earliest methods of food preservation was drying. Grains were sun- and air-dried to prevent mold growth and insect damage. Fruits and vegetables dried in the sun and meats dried and smoked over a fire were stored for use during times of need. Fruits were preserved by fermenting them into wines and vinegars, and fermented milk became curds, cheeses, and yogurts.

Methods of food preservation improved over the centuries, but there were severe limitations until the evolution of scientific methods made it possible to preserve food. By creating conditions unfavorable to the growth or survival of spoilage microorganisms and preventing deterioration by enzymes, scientists were able to extend the storage life of foods well beyond the normal period.

For most of history, people bought or traded for bulk foods, such as grain or rice, rather than prepared foods. This began to change in the early 1800s, when new methods of preserving and packaging foods

QUICK FACTS

School Subjects
Chemistry
Mathematics

Personal Skills
Communication/ideas
Technical/scientific

Work Environment
Primarily indoors
Primarily one location

Minimum Education Level
Bachelor's degree

Salary Range
$34,530 to $87,700 to $108,000+

Certification or Licensing
None available

Outlook
Faster than the average

DOT
041

GOE
02.03.04

NOC
2211

O*NET-SOC
19-1012.00, 19-4011.02

were developed. The science of food technology did not, however, really develop until shortly before the American entrance into World War II. Prompted by the need to supply U.S. troops with nutritious, flavorful foods that were not only easy to transport but also kept for long periods of time, scientists around 1940 began making great advances in the preparation, preservation, and packaging of foods. By the 1950s, food science and food technology departments were being established by many universities, and food science disciplines became important and respected areas of study.

Another boost to the food technology program came with the U.S. space program; new types of foods, as well as new types of preparation, packaging, and processing were needed to feed astronauts in space.

By the late 20th century, few people still canned or preserved their own fruits and vegetables. Advances in production methods in this century have made it possible to process larger quantities of a wider range of food products. Scientists specializing in food technology have found better ways to retard spoilage, improve flavor, and provide foods that are consistent in quality, flavor, texture, and size. Innovations such as freeze drying, irradiation, and artificial coloring and flavoring have changed the way many of the foods we eat are processed and prepared. Consumer demand for an ever-increasing variety of foods has created a demand for food technologists to develop them. Foods processed in a variety of ways are readily available to the consumer and have become such an accepted part of modern life that one rarely gives a thought to the complexities involved. The safety of the process, nutrition, development of new products and production methods, and the packaging of products are all the responsibility of food technologists.

THE JOB

Food technologists usually specialize in one phase of food technology. About one-third are involved in research and development. A large number are employed in quality-control laboratories or in the production or processing areas of food plants. Others teach or perform basic research in colleges and universities, work in sales or management positions, or are employed as technical writers or consultants. The branches of food technology are numerous and include cereal grains, meat and poultry, fats and oils, seafood, animal foods, beverages, dairy products, flavors, sugar and starches, stabilizers, preservatives, colors, and nutritional additives.

Food technologists in basic research study the structure and composition of food and observe the changes that take place during storage or processing. The knowledge they gain may enable them to develop new sources of proteins, determine the effects of processing on microorganisms, or isolate factors that affect the flavor, appearance, or texture of foods. Technologists engaged in applied research and development have the more practical task of creating new food products and developing new processing methods. They also continue to work with existing foods to make them more nutritious and flavorful and to improve their color and texture.

A rapidly growing area of food technology is biotechnology. Food technologists in this area work with plant breeding, gene splicing, microbial fermentation, and plant cell tissue cultures to produce enhanced raw products for processing.

Foods may lose their characteristics and nutritious value during processing and storage. Food technologists seek ways to prevent this by developing improved methods for processing, production, quality control, packaging, and distribution. They conduct chemical and microbiological tests on products to be sure they conform to standards set by the government and by the food industry. They also determine the nutritive content (the amounts of sugar, starch, protein, fat, vitamins, and minerals) that federal regulations say must be printed on the labels.

Food technologists in quality-control laboratories concentrate on ensuring that foods in every stage of processing meet industry and government standards. They check to see that raw ingredients are fresh, sufficiently ripe, and suitable for processing. They conduct periodic inspections of processing line operations. They also test after processing to be sure that various enzymes are not active and that bacteria levels are low enough so the food will not spoil or be unsafe to eat.

Some technologists test new products in test kitchens or develop new processing methods in laboratory pilot plants. Others devise new methods for packaging and storing foods. To solve problems, they may confer with processing engineers, flavor experts, or packaging and marketing specialists.

In processing plants, food technologists prepare production specifications and schedule processing operations. They ensure that proper temperature and humidity levels are maintained in storage areas and that wastes are disposed of properly and other sanitary regulations are observed throughout the plant. They also make recommendations to management in matters relating to efficiency or economy, such as new equipment or suppliers.

A food technologist *(left)* and plant pathologist collect cilantro samples after they have been washed. *(Peggy Greb, USDA, Agricultural Research Service)*

Some food technologists have positions in other fields where they can apply their specialized knowledge to such areas as advertising, market research, or technical sales. Others work as college educators.

REQUIREMENTS

High School

You can prepare for a career in food technology by taking plenty of high school science courses. Be sure to take biology, chemistry, and physics. To get hands-on experience working with food, take family and consumer science classes. Four years of mathematics classes, English classes, computer science classes, and other college-preparatory courses are also important to take.

Postsecondary Training

Educational requirements for this field are high. Beginners need at least a bachelor's degree in food technology, food science, or food engineering. Some technologists hold degrees in other areas, such as chemistry, biology, engineering, agriculture, or business, and nearly half have advanced degrees. Master's degrees and doctorates are mandatory for college teaching and are usually necessary for management and research positions.

More than 45 schools in the United States, Canada, and Mexico offer the course work needed to become a food technologist, and many of these programs have been approved by the Institute of Food Technologists. See the institute's Web site (http://www.ift.org) for approved school information. Typical courses include physics, biochemistry, mathematics, microbiology, the social sciences and humanities, and business administration as well as food technology courses, including food preservation, processing, sanitation, and marketing. Most of these schools also offer advanced degrees, usually in specialized areas of food technology. To successfully complete their program, candidates for a master's degree or a doctoral degree must perform extensive research and write a thesis reporting their original findings. Specialists in administrative, managerial, or regulatory areas may earn advanced degrees in business administration or in law rather than in food technology.

Other Requirements

Food technologists should have analytical minds and enjoy technical work. In addition, they must be able to express themselves clearly and be detail oriented. They also must be able to work well in group situations and participate and contribute to a team effort.

EXPLORING

Students may be able to arrange field trips to local food processing plants and plan interviews with or lectures by experts in the field. Apart from an interest in science, and especially chemistry, prospective food technologists may also develop interests in cooking and in inventing their own recipes.

Because of the educational requirements for food technologists, it is not likely that students will be able to acquire actual experience while still in high school. Part-time and summer employment as workers in food processing plants, however, would provide an excellent overview of the industry. More advanced college students may have opportunities for jobs helping out in research laboratories.

EMPLOYERS

There are approximately 13,400 food technologists employed in the United States. Food technologists work in a wide variety of settings, including food processing plants, food ingredient plants, and food manufacturing plants. They may work in basic research, product development, processing and quality assurance, packaging, or market research. There are positions in laboratories, test kitchens, and on production lines as well as with government agencies.

STARTING OUT

Many schools offering degree programs in food science will also offer job placement assistance. Also, recruiters from private industry frequently conduct interviews on campus. Faculty members may be willing to grant referrals to exceptional students. Another method is to make direct application to individual companies.

Frequently, the food products with which food technologists work determine where they are employed. Those who work with meats or grains may work in the Midwest. Technologists who work with citrus fruits usually work in Florida or California. Two-thirds of all food technologists are employed by private industry and the rest work for the federal government. Some major government employers of food technologists include the Environmental Protection Agency, National Aeronautics and Space Administration, the Food and Drug Administration, and the U.S. Department of Agriculture.

ADVANCEMENT

For food technologists with a bachelor's degree, there are two general paths to advancement, depending on whether they work in production or in research. They may begin as quality-assurance chemists or assistant production managers and, with experience, move up to more responsible management positions. Some technologists may start as junior food chemists in the research and development laboratory of a food company and advance to section head or another research management position.

Technologists who hold master's degrees may start out as food chemists in a research and development laboratory. Those with doctorates usually begin their careers in basic research or teaching. Other food technologists may gain expertise in more specialized areas and become sensory evaluation experts or food-marketing specialists.

EARNINGS

According to the U.S. Department of Labor (DOL), median annual earnings of food scientists and technologists were $59,630 in 2009. The highest paid workers earned more than $103,160, and the lowest paid earned less than $34,530.

The Institute of Food Technologists reports that its members earned a median salary of $87,700 in 2009. IFT members with a bachelor's degree in food science earned a median salary of $79,000. Members with a master's degree earned a median of $85,000, those with a Ph.D. earned a median of $103,000, and those with an M.B.A. earned a median of $108,000 a year.

Most food technologists receive generous benefit plans, which usually include health insurance, life insurance, pension plans, and vacation and sick pay. Others may receive funds for continuing education.

WORK ENVIRONMENT

Most food technologists work regular hours in clean, well-lighted, temperature-controlled offices, laboratories, or classrooms. Technologists in production and quality control who work in processing plants may be subject to machine noise and hot or cold conditions.

OUTLOOK

Employment for food technologists is expected to grow faster than the average for all careers through 2018, according to the DOL. The food industry is the largest single industry in the United States and throughout the world. Because people have to eat, there will always be a need for people to develop, test, and process food products. In developed countries, the ever-present consumer demand for new and different food products means that food scientists and technologists will always be in demand.

Several factors have also created continuing demand for skilled technologists. New labeling laws enacted in the 1990s have required companies to provide detailed nutritional information on their products. The continuing trend toward more healthful eating habits has recently focused on the roles of fats, cholesterol, and salt in nutrition, and companies have rushed to create a variety of low-fat, low-sodium, fat-free, cholesterol-free, and sodium-free foods. A larger and more varied supply of wholesome and economical food is needed to satisfy current tastes. The food industry will have to produce convenience foods of greater quality for use in homes and for the food service institutions that supply airlines, restaurants, and other major customers.

More technologists may be hired to research and produce new foods from modifications of wheat, corn, rice, and soybeans, such as the "meat" products made from vegetable proteins. The food industry has increased its spending in recent years for this kind of research and development and is likely to continue to do so. Developing these products, without sacrificing such important factors as taste, appearance, and texture, has produced many new opportunities for food technologists. Food technologists will also be sought to produce new foods for poor and starving people in underdeveloped countries. Experienced technologists will use their advanced training to create new foods from such staples as rice, corn, wheat, and soybeans.

An increasing focus on food safety and biosecurity will also create demand for food technologists with knowledge of these practice areas. Growth will also occur for food technologists who are trained to use biotechnology and nanotechnology to test and monitor food quality.

Finally, the increasing emphasis on the automation of many elements of food processing has also created a need for food technologists to adapt cooking and preparation processes to the new technology.

FOR MORE INFORMATION

For consumer fact sheets, information on issues in the food science industry, and food safety news, visit the association's Web site or contact
Grocery Manufacturers Association
1350 I Street, NW, Suite 300
Washington, DC 20005-3377
Tel: 202-639-5900
E-mail: info@gmaonline.org
http://www.gmaonline.org

For information on accredited food science programs and food science careers, visit the IFT Web site.
Institute of Food Technologists (IFT)
525 West Van Buren, Suite 1000
Chicago, IL 60607-3830
Tel: 312-782-8424
E-mail: info@ift.org
http://www.ift.org

For national news on agriculture and food issues, contact
U.S. Department of Agriculture
1400 Independence Avenue, SW
Washington, DC 20250-0002

Tel: 202-720-2791
http://www.usda.gov

For *information on food safety, contact*
U.S. Food and Drug Administration
10903 New Hampshire Avenue
Silver Spring, MD 20993-0002
Tel: 888-463-6332
http://www.fda.gov

For *information and activities that explore the science behind cook-ing, visit*
The Accidental Scientist: The Science of Cooking
http://www.exploratorium.edu/cooking

For *comprehensive information on careers, educational programs, and scholarships, visit*
Careers in Food Science
http://school.discovery.com/foodscience/college_resources.html

INTERVIEW

Dr. Ruth MacDonald, *professor and chair of the Department of Food Science and Human Nutrition at Iowa State University in Ames, Iowa, discussed food science education with the editors of* Careers in Focus: Agriculture.

Q. Can you please tell us about the programs that are offered by your department?

A.

Food Science

- Food science and technology: This curriculum is approved by the Institute of Food Technologists (IFT). It is designed for students who wish to go to graduate or professional school or who are biotechnology scholars. Preveterinary prepara-tion is available.
- Food science and industry: This curriculum is approved by the IFT, and the program combines food science and busi-ness courses to prepare students for the sales/management part of the food industry.
- Consumer food science: This curriculum emphasizes the relationship between food science, food preparation, and consumers' concerns about nutritional quality; it is designed for students interested in test kitchen positions, food

product formulation and recipe development, food promotion, and consumer services.

Nutritional Science

Graduates of this degree program have a strong basic science education along with human nutrition expertise, which enables them to work in nutrition research laboratories, pursue graduate study in nutrition or related areas, and/or pursue health professional school admission. This curriculum can serve as a program for nutritional graduate study or as a prehealth professional program such as medicine, pharmacy, dentistry, veterinary medicine, physical therapy, occupational therapy, optometry, ophthalmology, physician assistant, podiatry, optometry, or nurse practitioner. Students pursuing a preprofessional program of study are encouraged to contact the admissions counselor at the university where they plan to complete their practice degree to determine specific course requirements.

Dietetics

The undergraduate didactic program in dietetics is approved by the American Dietetic Association. Graduates are eligible to apply for admission to dietetic internships/supervised practice programs. Upon successful completion of the experience program, graduates are eligible to take the national examination to become a registered dietitian.

Q. Are internship opportunities available to students at your school?

A. No formal internships are required for our food science students, although we have many that do participate in internships. Typically, food science students work in the food industry during the summer months as interns. We also have some nutrition students that work in the food industry.

Q. What is one thing that young people may not know about a career in food science?

A. That this degree provides many great career opportunities with a diversity of content and responsibilities. There are many high-paying positions for food scientists in industry, with great growth potential. Students may have to spend some time doing a job that is not their ideal, but will lead to a more challenging position within a company.

Q. For what type of jobs does your program prepare students?

A. All types of positions in food processing and manufacturing, food quality assurance, and food safety. We also prepare students for academic positions at the graduate level.

Q. What are the most important personal and professional qualities for food science majors?

A. Students should expect to have a high level of technical skills, which they acquire through course work. Excellent verbal and written communication skills are absolutely necessary. The ability to solve complex problems, which comes from integration of critical thinking skills, is also of critical importance.

Q. What is the employment outlook for food scientists?

A. Excellent—all of our students find good jobs, and we usually have employers seeking students to hire. The IFT has done several studies that indicate a shortage of qualified food scientists in the next few years, so the market is looking very good.

Q. Are there any changes in this job market that students should expect?

A. Increased focus on global markets, integration of human health in the food industry, and the impact of security (terrorism) on the food industry will be important in the future. More food-related industries are becoming larger conglomerates, which impacts the nature of the positions as well.

Q. Have certain areas of this field been especially promising in recent years?

A. Increased focus on traceability issues (security) and monitoring the ingredient flow is becoming critical. There is a focus on more understanding of nutrition and health to be able to take advantage of the consumer demand for these products. New processing technologies such as high-pressure processing and radiation and thermal treatments have also emerged.

Grain Merchants

QUICK FACTS

School Subjects
Business
Mathematics

Personal Skills
Leadership/management
Mechanical/manipulative

Work Environment
Primarily indoors
Primarily multiple locations

Minimum Education Level
Bachelor's degree

Salary Range
$30,250 to $53,150 to
$101,480+

Certification or Licensing
None available (certification)
Required for certain positions (licensing)

Outlook
Little or no change

DOT
162

GOE
13.02.02

NOC
6411

O*NET-SOC
13-1021.00

OVERVIEW

Grain merchants buy grain from farms and sell it to consumers. Between the buying and the selling, they are concerned with the quality, market value, shipping, processing, and storing of the grain. In effect, they are liaisons between the farmer and the eventual user or consumer of the grain. The regulation activities of the grain merchant create an efficient market for grain around the world. Grain merchants work as either *grain buyers* or *grain managers*. The U.S. Department of Labor (DOL) classifies grain merchants under the general career "purchasing agents and buyers, farm products." There are approximately 14,100 purchasing agents and buyers of farm products employed in the United States.

HISTORY

Trading grain in the past was relatively simple. Farmers sold their wheat, corn, oats, barley, and rice in the public market in their town. People bought enough grain to meet their families' needs, and farmers purchased grain for their animals. As grain production grew, firms that purchased, stored, processed, and transported grains were established. In certain cities with good transportation facilities, such as Chicago and Kansas City, grain exchanges where grain merchants could buy and sell their commodities were established.

Today the buying and selling of grain is a complicated process involving farmers, merchants, food processors, and consumers. Grain merchants have played a vital role in making this process more efficient. Farmers, unlike factories, can only harvest their crops when they are ripe, but consumers need their produce all year round. By purchasing, processing, transporting, and storing grain until other buyers can be found, grain merchants facilitate the smooth flow of the commodity all year round, during times of both shortages and surpluses. This results in a fair market price for the farmer and a steady supply of food for the consumer.

THE JOB

Grain elevators are structures that resemble silos where grain is stored and sold. They are a common sight in the agricultural and livestock regions of the Midwest, South, and Southwest. Grain merchants do most of their buying at the local grain elevator, where they meet with area farmers and try to negotiate a fair price. The grain elevator, which may be privately or cooperatively owned, then sells its grain to the terminal elevators located in cities with good transportation access, such as Chicago, Minneapolis, Omaha, Kansas City, and Fort Worth.

Grain merchants must have good instincts about when it will be most profitable to purchase grain. They may buy grain when the supply they have on hand reaches a predetermined reorder point, when a person or company specially orders it, or when market conditions are especially favorable. When purchasing grain, merchants must consider the type of grain specified, its market price, quantity discounts, freight handling or other transportation costs, and delivery time. Much of this information can be obtained by comparing listings in catalogs and trade journals, interviewing

Grain Elevators

The Country Grain Elevator Historical Society evolved to preserve the small country grain elevator. Early in the 20th century, wood crib elevators cropped up along the railway lines as small farming communities prospered. Today, many of the elevators have been abandoned because of obsolete equipment, or destroyed because of the threat of liability. To visit an archive of photos and documents, visit the society's Web site (http://www.country-grain-elevator-historical-society.org). You can also contact the society by writing to 155 Prospector Trail, Bozeman, MT 59718-7988, e-mailing bselyem@country-grain-elevator-historical-society.org, or calling 406-388-9282.

suppliers' representatives, keeping up with current market trends, and examining samples. Many grain merchants are dependent on computers for online access to up-to-date price listings or programs that keep track of inventory levels and process routine orders.

Merchants must be sufficiently familiar with the various qualities of grain to determine whether to purchase certain grains. They inspect samples of grain by weighing them, checking their moisture content, and examining them for insects or other damage. Grain must also be classified according to type. The U.S. Department of Agriculture (USDA) has developed grain standards to ensure that grains of a certain grade from all over the country meet the same specifications. After merchants make an initial appraisal of the quality of the grain, they send samples to a federal grain inspector for an official appraisal.

Although grain merchants often are involved in many aspects of the buying, storing, and reselling process, there are two major specialists who perform different functions in this occupation.

Grain buyers evaluate and purchase grain for resale and milling. They select the type of grain to order based on current demand and possible future considerations. Grain buyers arrange for the transportation and storage of the grain and identify possible resale markets. They hope to make money by reselling the grain for a higher price than they paid for it. They either buy the grain themselves, hoping to sell it in the near future, or buy and sell for businesses, making a commission on each sale.

Buyers must keep up-to-date on all information that affects grain and grain prices. In making purchasing decisions they must take into account the weather, planting schedules, consumer trends, crop qualities, and government standards both in the United States and abroad.

Because of market fluctuations in the price of grains, holding on to grain for any length of time is risky. To minimize their risk, buyers may purchase commodity futures, which are agreements to buy or sell an amount of grain at a future date. These futures are hedges against changes in the price of grain. Later the buyers sell their supply of grain to a food processor or grain exporter and buy back their hedges.

Grain managers work at terminal elevators or other holding facilities. Managers must inspect all the grain that comes to the holding terminal and calculate its market value. In estimating its market value, managers look at moisture content, protein, oil, damage, and the presence of live insects, as well as costs for transportation and handling. They may also send samples to federal grain inspection agencies for a government standardized analysis.

Managers keep daily records on the kinds and grades of grain received, prices paid, amount purchased, and the amount in storage. They also supervise grain elevator workers in the unloading, loading, storing, and mixing of the grain for shipment and milling.

REQUIREMENTS

High School

You should take classes in business, accounting, history, and economics to get a sense of world markets and trading. English and composition courses will help you develop communication skills needed for working with farmers, managers, and other agribusiness professionals. Mathematics classes will help you prepare for the accounting, calculating, and analysis involved in this work. If your high school offers courses in agriculture, take those that will teach you about crop production. Other classes that will give you an understanding of plant growth and the environment include earth science, biology, and chemistry.

Postsecondary Training

Though you may be able to get some assistant positions with only a high school diploma, many grain merchants have undergraduate or graduate degrees in agriculture, economics, or business management from a college or university. However, two-year programs can also be beneficial. In either case, the prospective grain merchant should take courses in agricultural economics, accounting, purchasing, finance, and business law. As finances in the agricultural sector tighten and some farmers go out of business, future grain merchants will probably deal with fewer, more specialized farms.

Certification or Licensing

Grain merchants in commodity futures, who deal directly with the public, must be licensed by the federal government. They must also meet a code of ethics and a series of guidelines set up to test their skills.

Other Requirements

In order to be successful, you must have an excellent rapport with farmers and other suppliers. This relationship determines whether you'll be able to get a good price on the grain, favorable payment terms, quick delivery on emergency orders, or help in obtaining the grain during times of scarcity. To negotiate these and other conditions, you must have good communications skills, be able to work effectively with others, and handle high-pressure situations. You must be persuasive, diplomatic, and cooperative. As with most business jobs, one gets ahead with initiative, dependability, good judgment, and trustworthiness.

EXPLORING

If you live in an agricultural community with grain elevators, you might be able to find part-time or seasonal work with a farming cooperative or other grain purchasing organization. It may also be possible to get part-time work at a commodities exchange to learn about the profession from that angle. In addition, some school work-study programs provide opportunities for part-time, on-the-job training with grain elevators. Reading industry periodicals such as *Farm Journal* (http://www.agweb.com/farmjournal) and *Grain Journal* (http://www.grainnet.com) will give you insight into the business concerns of grain merchants. Also, consider joining your school's branch of the National FFA Organization to learn more about the role of agriculture in today's society.

EMPLOYERS

Approximately 14,100 purchasing agents and buyers of farm products are employed in the United States. Grain merchants may work in local grain elevators in agricultural communities or with the corporate headquarters of major grain companies. They also find work in commodities exchanges. Companies that supply products and equipment to grain processing companies hire people with elevator management and agribusiness experience. The USDA and other government agencies also hire grain merchants; the USDA Grain Inspection, Packers, and Stockyards Administration sponsors many projects that require grain professionals.

STARTING OUT

A good college program will include internship opportunities, as well as career placement services. Jobs with grain elevators will be advertised in the newspaper; entry-level positions include grain elevator worker and commodities exchange clerk. With some experience, you can move into an assistant manager or assistant operator position. The Grain Elevator and Processing Society serves as the professional organization for grain professionals and sponsors annual conventions and other opportunities for members to network with others in the industry.

ADVANCEMENT

A skilled grain merchant may become a grain elevator manager or a grain buyer for a large company. As always, those with the most training and experience stand the best prospects of advancing to positions of higher pay and greater responsibility. Changing employers is another way to advance in this field. Some skilled grain merchants become consultants for the federal government or take a similar position with a bank, insurance company, or other private company.

EARNINGS

As with other brokers, some grain merchants work on a commission basis and others work for a straight salary. Earnings vary depending on the size of the employer, the experience of the employee, and the specific job responsibilities. The DOL reports that the median salary for purchasing agents and buyers of farm products was $53,150 in 2009. The lowest paid 10 percent earned less than $30,250 and the highest paid 10 percent earned more than $101,480 a year.

Salaries, overall, are highest for elevator managers at large regional terminals and for successful grain buyers and brokers. While grain brokers and commodities traders can earn quite a bit of money, the nature of their work means they could lose huge amounts as well. A great deal of a grain merchant's success depends on making the proper contacts with grain suppliers and buyers. Those who work for the federal government may earn somewhat less than those in the private sector. Full-time grain merchants usually receive paid holidays, health insurance, and other benefits. Many firms also have pension plans.

WORK ENVIRONMENT

The work environment of a grain merchant can vary from a typical office setting to the drama of a trading room floor. It is a profession that often requires taking great risks and as a result, receiving great rewards or great disappointments.

Grain merchants generally work a standard week of 37 to 40 hours, although overtime is likely in situations when grain supplies are in demand or in a state of flux. Some grain merchants, especially grain buyers, travel a great deal. These trips are necessary to buy and sell grain, make any necessary inspections, and keep in contact with current and prospective clients. Those who travel are usually reimbursed for expenses incurred for lodging, transportation, and other necessities.

OUTLOOK

Little or no change in employment is expected for purchasing agents and buyers of farm products through 2018, according to the DOL. Despite this prediction, there will continue to be some new jobs for grain merchants. Since grain must be evaluated for freshness and quality, it is not as easy to conduct transactions for this product electronically.

The populations of small agricultural communities are rapidly decreasing in some parts of the country, particularly in the Plains states. However, even though many of the grain elevators are closing in these areas as farmers look for more stable sources of income, grain is still in great demand around the world. Agribusiness professionals, consultants, and the U.S. government are all involved in increasing this demand by searching for new, efficient uses for grain. Scientific advances will also aid in the storage and processing of grain.

A number of issues affect the grain industry every year, and results are often difficult to predict. Grain production and sales are influenced by weather, planting seasons, and the overseas market. In addition, the technological development of genetically modified grains has lead to increased production but also resulted in grain products that are impossible to sell in some markets. The railroad industry can also affect grain sales; if there aren't enough rail cars available to haul the grain away, elevators with limited storage and excess grain are forced to pile the grain on the ground. Decisions by government agencies such as the USDA and the Environmental Protection Agency also determine the way grain merchants do business. Laws concerning emissions standards and storage facilities sometimes call for costly repairs and down time.

FOR MORE INFORMATION

To learn about current issues affecting grain companies and their employees, contact

Grain Elevator and Processing Society
4248 Park Glen Road
Minneapolis, MN 55416-4758
Tel: 952-928-4640
E-mail: info@geaps.com
http://www.geaps.com

To learn about the government's role in the marketing of grain,
contact
Grain Inspection, Packers, and Stockyards Administration
http://www.gipsa.usda.gov/GISPA

For information on the agricultural industry, contact
U.S. Department of Agriculture
1400 Independence Avenue, SW
Washington, DC 20250-0002
Tel: 202-720-2791
http://www.usda.gov

Horticultural Inspectors

QUICK FACTS

School Subjects
Agriculture
Biology
Health

Personal Skills
Communication/ideas
Technical/scientific

Work Environment
Indoors and outdoors
Primarily multiple locations

Minimum Education Level
Bachelor's degree

Salary Range
$24,670 to $41,500 to
$60,460+

Certification or Licensing
Required for certain
positions

Outlook
About as fast as the average

DOT
168

GOE
04.04.02

NOC
2263

O*NET-SOC
45-2011.00

OVERVIEW

Horticultural inspectors are employed by federal, state, and local governments to enforce those laws that protect public health and safety as they pertain to plants and agricultural products. Approximately 16,600 agricultural inspectors are employed in the United States.

HISTORY

Federal, state, and local laws have been enacted to provide protection to citizens in many areas of daily life, including horticultural production, storage, and transportation. Over the years, federal, state, and local governments have developed a system of regular inspection and reporting to assure these safety standards are maintained.

Rather than wait until a law has been violated, it is more efficient to employ horticultural inspectors to continuously monitor the way in which standards requirements are carried out. Horticultural inspectors enforce compliance with all health and safety laws and regulations that are related to agriculture and horticulture.

THE JOB

Because there are so many areas of horticulture and food production that require regulation, there are different types of specialists within the field of horticultural inspection who determine the best way to comply with laws. The following paragraphs describe some of the major kinds of horticultural inspectors employed by the government.

Agricultural chemicals inspectors inspect establishments where agricultural service products such as fertilizers, pesticides, and livestock feed and medications are manufactured, marketed, and used. They may monitor distribution warehouses, retail outlets, processing plants, and private and industrial farms to collect samples of their products for analysis. If there is a violation, they gather information and samples for use as legal evidence.

Agricultural-chemical registration specialists review and evaluate information on pesticides, fertilizers, and other products containing dangerous chemicals. If the manufacturers or distributors of the products have complied with government regulations, their applications for registration are approved.

Agricultural commodity graders ensure that retailers and consumers get reliable and safe commodities. They may specialize in cotton, dairy products, eggs and egg products, processed or fresh fruit or vegetables, or grains. The inspectors check product standards and issue official grading certificates. They also verify sanitation standards by means of regular inspection of plants and equipment.

Agriculture specialists work to protect crops, forests, gardens, and livestock from the introduction and spread of plant pests and animal diseases. They act as agricultural experts at ports of entry to help protect people from agroterrorism and bioterrorism, as well as monitor agricultural imports for diseases and harmful pests. They inspect aircraft, ships, railway cars, and other transportation entering the United States for restricted or prohibited plant or animal materials. They also work to prevent the spread of agricultural disease from one state or one part of the country to another.

Disease and insect control field inspectors inspect fields to detect the presence of harmful insects and plant diseases. Inspectors count the numbers of insects on plants or of diseased plants within a sample area. They record the results of their counts on field work sheets. They also collect samples of unidentifiable insects or diseased plants for identification by a supervisor.

Environmental health inspectors, also called *sanitarians,* work primarily for state and local governments to ensure that government standards of cleanliness and purity are met in food, water, and air. They may inspect processing plants, dairies, restaurants, hospitals, and other institutions. Environmental health inspectors in state or local agricultural or health departments may specialize in milk and dairy production, water or air pollution, food or institutional sanitation, or occupational health.

Nursery inspectors work primarily for state and local governments to ensure that nurseries, greenhouses, and garden centers sell disease-free plants, trees, shrubs, and other products. They inspect plants that are imported from other countries, as well as any plants that may be shipped abroad or out of state. Nursery inspectors are knowledgeable about a wide variety of plant pests such as Japanese beetles, gypsy moths, pine shoot beetles, emerald ash borers, and others, as well as plant diseases such as sudden oak death. They also make sure that nurseries have the proper licensing and that workers meet all labor standards established by the U.S. Department of Labor (DOL) and other federal, state, local regulating agencies.

REQUIREMENTS

There is such a variety of skills involved in these inspection jobs that the qualifications and education required depend on the area of work.

High School

The minimum education required to be a horticultural inspector is generally a bachelor's degree. High school students should focus on college preparatory classes in speech; English, especially writing; business; computer science; and general mathematics. They should also focus on biology, health, chemistry, agriculture, earth science, and shop or vocational training.

Postsecondary Training

The specific degree and training qualifications vary for each position and area in which inspection is done. For federal positions, a civil service examination is generally required. Education and experience in the specific field is usually necessary. College courses in agricultural science, biology, government, or related subjects will also be useful for aspiring agricultural inspectors.

Certification or Licensing

Certification and licensing requirements vary according to the position. Contact the agency for which you would like to work for detailed information on certification and licensing.

Other Requirements

Horticultural inspectors must be precision-minded, have an eye for detail, and be able to accept responsibility. They must be tenacious and patient as they follow each case from investigation to its conclusion. They also must be able to communicate well with others in order to reach a clear analysis of a situation and be able to report this information to a superior or coworker. Inspectors must be able to write effective reports that convey vast amounts of information and investigative work.

EXPLORING

If you are interested in work as a horticultural inspector, you should read books and magazines about agriculture. You can also learn more by talking with people who are employed as inspectors and with your high school career counselor. Employment in a specific field during summer vacations could be valuable preparation and an opportunity to determine if a general field, such as horticulture, is of interest to you.

EMPLOYERS

There are approximately 16,600 agricultural inspectors employed in the United States. The federal government employs the majority of inspectors in certain areas, such as food and agriculture, which fall under the U.S. Public Health Service, the U.S. Department of Agriculture, or the U.S. Department of Homeland Security. Consumer safety is evenly divided between local government and the U.S. Food and Drug Administration.

STARTING OUT

Applicants may enter the occupation by applying to take the appropriate civil service examinations. Education in specific areas may be required. Some positions require a degree or other form of training. Others need considerable on-the-job experience in the field.

   The civil service commissions for state and local employment will provide information on health and regulatory inspection positions under their jurisdiction. The federal government provides information on available jobs at local offices of the employment service or at the U.S. Office of Personnel Management's Web site, http://www .usajobs.opm.gov. The specific agency concerned with a job area can also be contacted.

ADVANCEMENT

Advancement for horticultural inspectors in the federal government is based on the civil service promotion and salary structure. Advancement is automatic, usually at one-year intervals, for those people whose work is satisfactory. Additional education may also contribute to advancement to supervisory positions.

Advancements for horticultural inspectors in state and local government and in private industry are often similar to those offered at the federal level.

EARNINGS

According to the DOL, horticultural inspectors earned median wages of $41,500 in 2009. Earnings ranged from less than $24,670 to $60,460 or more annually. Horticultural inspectors for state and local governments generally earn salaries lower than those paid by the federal government.

Horticultural inspectors also receive other benefits including paid vacation and sick days, health and dental insurance, pensions, and life insurance. Most inspectors enjoy the use of an official automobile and reimbursement for travel expenses.

WORK ENVIRONMENT

Most horticultural inspectors should expect to travel a considerable amount of the time. They will interact with a wide variety of people from different educational and professional backgrounds. Horticultural inspectors sometimes work long and irregular hours. Sometimes, inspectors will experience stressful, unpleasant, and even dangerous situations. Agricultural and food inspection may bring contact with unpleasant odors, loud noises, potentially infectious diseases, and other difficult working conditions. Agricultural commodity graders may work outside in the heat or in cool refrigeration units. They may also be required to lift heavy objects.

Inspectors may face adversarial situations with individuals or organizations that feel that they do not warrant an investigation, are above the law, or are being singled out for inspection.

The work of horticultural inspectors is important and can be rewarding. Compensation and job security are generally good, and travel and automobile expenses are reimbursed when necessary. Inspectors can be proud that the skilled performance of their duties improves life in some way or another for every member of our society.

OUTLOOK

Employment of inspectors is projected to grow about as fast as the average for all occupations through 2018 as a result of the public's concern for safe and healthy food products. The threat of agroterrorism and bioterrorism and recent national outbreaks of food poisoning have reinforced the need for qualified horticultural inspectors.

FOR MORE INFORMATION

For career information, visit the CBP Web site.
U.S. Customs and Border Protection (CBP)
U.S. Department of Homeland Security
1300 Pennsylvania Avenue, NW
Washington, DC 20229-0002
Tel: 877-227-5511
http://www.cbp.gov

For information on farm policies, homeland security issues, and other news relating to the agricultural industry, visit the USDA Web site.
U.S. Department of Agriculture (USDA)
1400 Independence Avenue, SW
Washington, DC 20250-0002
Tel: 202-720-2791
http://www.usda.gov

Horticultural Technicians

QUICK FACTS

School Subjects
Agriculture
Biology
Earth science

Personal Skills
Artistic
Technical/scientific

Work Environment
Indoors and outdoors
Primarily multiple locations

Minimum Education Level
High school diploma

Salary Range
$15,080 to $23,480 to
$41,600+

Certification or Licensing
Required by certain states

Outlook
Faster than the average

DOT
405

GOE
03.02.01, 03.03.04

NOC
2225

O*NET-SOC
37-3011.00, 37-3012.00,
37-3013.00, 45-2092.00,
45-2092.01

OVERVIEW

Horticultural technicians cultivate and market plants and flowers that make human surroundings more beautiful. They plant and care for ground cover and trees in parks, on playgrounds, along public highways, and in other areas. They also landscape public and private lands. There are approximately 1.5 million people employed in landscape and horticultural services.

HISTORY

Planting and cultivating gardens is an ancient art form. The famed hanging gardens of Babylon, the formal gardens of Athens, and the terraces and geometric gardens of Italy are early examples of this art. Historically, different countries were renowned for the different types of gardens they cultivated. For instance, Holland distinguished itself by growing dozens of varieties of tulips, and France was known for its fantastic royal gardens. In the 18th century, gardens became more informal and natural, typified by the plantings around George Washington's home, Mount Vernon. In the United States, the first large landscaped area was New York City's Central Park, created in the 1850s. While flowers, parks, and gardens are not as common in the United States as in other countries, a growing enthusiasm is creating a new demand for trained horticultural technicians.

THE JOB

Horticultural technicians usually specialize in one or more of the following areas: floriculture (flowers), nursery operation (shrubs, hedges, and trees), turfgrass (grass), and arboriculture (trees). Most entry-level technicians work as growers, maintenance workers, or salespeople.

The activities of *floriculture technicians* and of *nursery-operation technicians* are closely related. Both kinds of technicians work in nurseries or greenhouses to raise and sell plants. They determine correct soil conditions for specific plants, the proper rooting material for cuttings, and the best fertilizer for promoting growth. They may also be involved with the merchandising aspects of growing plants.

Technicians working in floriculture or nursery operations may become *horticultural-specialty growers* or *plant propagators*. These technicians initiate new kinds of plant growth through specialized techniques both in outdoor fields and under the environmentally controlled conditions of greenhouses and growing sheds. They carefully plan growing schedules, quantities, and utilization schemes to gain the highest quality and most profitable yield. Some of their duties include planting seeds, transplanting seedlings, pruning plants, and inspecting crops for nutrient deficiencies, insects, diseases, and unwanted growth.

In greenhouses and growing sheds, horticultural-specialty growers monitor timing and metering devices that administer nutrients to the plants and flowers. They also regulate humidity, ventilation, and carbon dioxide conditions, often using computer programs. They formulate schedules for the dispensing of herbicides, fungicides, and pesticides and explain and demonstrate growing techniques and procedures to other workers. Horticultural-specialty growers may also hire personnel, work with vendors and customers, and handle record keeping.

Horticultural technicians working in the area of turf-grass management are involved in the planning and maintenance of commercial lawns and public lands, such as parks, highways, and playing fields. They also work in specialized areas, such as sod production, seed production, irrigation, transportation, and sales of other products and services.

Turfgrass technicians may run their own businesses or work for lawn care services. Private businesses provide lawn care services to homeowners, corporations, colleges, and other large institutions with extensive grounds. These services include mowing, fertilizing, irrigating, and controlling insects, diseases, and weeds. They also may provide tree and snow removal services and sell lawn care products and equipment. Technicians working in the public sector for local, county, state, or federal government agencies may be involved in designing turfgrass areas in parks or playing fields, or for areas along public highways.

Arboriculture technicians plant, feed, prune, and provide pest control for trees. Self-employed technicians may contract their services to private businesses or a group of companies located in the same industrial park or neighborhood. They care for the trees on the company grounds or in the landscaped areas of industrial parks. Private companies hire arboriculture technicians not only to keep their grounds attractive but also to prevent damage by fallen trees or overgrowth to on-site power lines or other property.

Arboriculture technicians are also employed by local, state, or federal agencies. They decide when and how trees should be removed and where new trees should be placed on public grounds. They work for park and parkway systems, public recreational agencies, and public school systems.

REQUIREMENTS

High School

Many entry-level jobs, especially in landscaping and turf grass management, are available out of high school. For these positions, the majority of training takes place on the job. To prepare yourself in high school, take any agricultural classes available, particularly those that include units in botany. Science courses, such as biology, chemistry, and earth science, will also teach you about plant life, development, and the effects of various nutrients. Math, business, and accounting classes will be valuable if you're considering working in retail sales, or running your own business. Also, take English and composition courses to improve your communication skills for preparing reports and assisting in research.

Postsecondary Training

For management and more technical positions, most employers prefer applicants who have an associate's degree in applied science. Many horticulture training programs are available across the country. Programs include horticulture courses in landscape plants, pest management, nursery management, and plant propagation. In addition, students take courses in English composition, small business management, and agribusiness.

National FFA Organization

In 1928, teachers, students, and agricultural business owners met in Kansas City in support of agricultural education and founded the Future Farmers of America. Since then, the group, now known as the National FFA Organization, has been a driving force in helping students develop leadership skills and find career success through agricultural education.

Middle and high school-age students enrolled in an agricultural course can join a National FFA Organization chapter at their schools or join nearby chapters. Members can receive scholarships, participate in competitions, receive career advice and hands-on leadership training, and participate in many other activities. Among the variety of programs offered by the National FFA Organization is FFA Global. Activities in this program include virtual tours and travel programs, which help young people interested in agriculture connect with their peers throughout the world. Visit https://www.ffa.org for more information.

Certification or Licensing

Though there are no national certification standards, many states require certification for workers who apply pesticides. Other states require landscape contractors to obtain a license.

Voluntary certification is available to those who want increased opportunities or to advance their career. The Professional Landcare Network offers the following certification designations: landscape industry certified technician-interior, landscape industry certified technician-exterior, landscape industry certified manager, landscape industry certified horticultural technician, landscape industry certified ornamental maintenance technician, landscape industry certified lawn care manager, and landscape industry certified lawn care technician. Other organizations, such as the Professional Grounds Management Society (see the end of this article for contact information), offer additional levels of certification based on education and experience levels.

Other Requirements

To enjoy and succeed in horticulture, you should have an eye for aesthetic beauty and a love of nature. Creative and artistic talents help in arranging flowers in a retail setting or organizing plants in a garden or greenhouse. Horticultural technicians must also possess people skills, as they work closely with professionals as well as clients. If running their own business, technicians need to be detail oriented, self-motivated, and organized.

EXPLORING

If you've spent a summer mowing lawns for your family or neighbors or kept up a garden in the backyard, then you already have valuable horticulture experience. Many nurseries, flower shops, and local parks or forest preserves use temporary summer employees to work in various capacities. You can also join garden clubs, visit local flower shops, and attend botanical shows to explore the career. The American Public Gardens Association offers internships in public gardens throughout the United States (see the end of this article for contact information).

If you are between the ages of five and 22, you might also want to join the National Junior Horticultural Association, which offers horticulture-related projects, contests, and other activities. Visit http://www.njha.org for more information.

EMPLOYERS

Approximately 1.5 million workers are employed in landscaping, groundskeeping, nursery, greenhouse, and lawn services. The variety of jobs available within the horticultural field provides a number of opportunities. Employers include local parks and recreation departments, botanical gardens, college research facilities, grounds maintenance crews, greenhouses, and lawn care businesses. Sales positions are available for knowledgeable technicians in floral shops, garden stores, and nurseries. Many horticultural technicians are self-employed and run their own lawn care services and greenhouses.

STARTING OUT

Horticulture training programs often offer job placement or internship services. Internships, in turn, may lead to full-time positions with the same employer. Check the classified section of your local newspaper for openings, including those in many chain grocery, hardware, and drugstores with greenhouses and plant departments.

ADVANCEMENT

Nursery operation and floriculture technicians may advance to a management position in a garden center, greenhouse, flower shop, or other related retail business. These managers are responsible for the entire operation of a retail or wholesale outlet or a specific department. They maintain inventories; interact with customers and suppliers; hire, train, and supervise employees; direct advertising and promotion activities; and keep records and accounts. Technicians also advance to work as *horticultural inspectors,* who work for local, state, or federal governments. Arboriculture technicians find opportunities as garden superintendents, tree surgeons, and park supervisors. Turfgrass technicians may advance to such positions as grounds superintendent, commercial sod grower, consultant, or park/golf course supervisor.

With additional experience and education (usually a degree from a four-year institution), some floriculture and nursery-operation technicians become *horticulturists,* either at a research facility or a large firm. Horticulturists conduct experiments and investigations into problems of breeding, production, storage, processing, and transit of fruits, nuts, berries, vegetables, flowers, bushes, and trees. They develop new plant varieties and determine methods of planting, spraying, cultivating, and harvesting.

Many advancement opportunities in this field require technicians to start their own businesses. This requires sufficient funds and the willingness to commit one's own financial resources to career development.

EARNINGS

Because of the wide range of jobs available to horticultural technicians, average hourly salaries vary from minimum wage to more than $20 an hour (which translates into approximately $15,080 to $41,600 or more per year). According to U.S. Department of Labor (DOL) data, in 2009 landscaping and groundskeeping workers earned an average of $11.29 an hour (approximately $23,480 annually for full-time work). With more experience, managers of landscaping, lawn service, and groundskeeping workers earned an average of $19.69 an hour (approximately $40,950 annually). Fringe benefits vary from employer to employer, but generally include hospitalization and other insurance coverage, retirement benefits, and educational assistance. Self-employed workers, however, have to provide their own benefits.

WORK ENVIRONMENT

Horticultural technicians generally work a 40-hour week. Those who work in parks are often required to work weekends and some summer evenings. Whether working indoors in a greenhouse or florist shop, or outdoors in a park or on a golf course, they are surrounded by beauty. However, the job comes in all kinds of weather. Arboriculture technicians, landscape developers, and turfgrass technicians spend a good deal of time outdoors and occasionally must work in rain, mud, or extreme temperatures.

Some technicians, such as those who work in greenhouses, public gardens, and floral shops, work in fairly peaceful surroundings and are able to enjoy the products of their work—the flowers or plants they tend. Jobs can also be exhausting and strenuous. Depending on the job, workers may have to climb trees, lift large equipment, mow large lawns, or kneel and bend to care for plants and soil. Some of the machinery used, such as blower vacs and mowers, can be very noisy. In addition, depending on the nature of the work, technicians may have to handle chemicals.

OUTLOOK

Employment for horticultural technicians is expected to grow faster than the average for all occupations through 2018, according to the DOL. High turnover in the business continually provides openings. Many horticultural technicians work only part time, so employers are often looking to fill vacant positions. Because wages for beginning workers are low, employers have difficulty attracting enough workers.

The continued development and redevelopment of urban areas, such as the construction of commercial and industrial buildings, shopping malls, homes, highways, and parks, contribute to the steady growth of employment opportunities for horticulture technicians. An increased interest in lawn care and the environment also has created a demand for skilled workers. There is a wider public awareness of the benefits of lawn care, such as safer yards for children to play in, more attractive surroundings for family relaxation and entertaining, and increased home value. To care for their property while conserving leisure time, homeowners are expected to continue to use professional lawn care services.

On the other hand, many homeowners like to care for their landscaping themselves. To cater to this consumer, many retail chain stores, from drugstores to hardware stores, greatly expand their lawn and garden centers every spring and summer and need knowledgeable horticultural workers on staff.

FOR MORE INFORMATION

To learn more about special gardening programs, and to get other information about public gardens, contact

American Public Gardens Association
351 Longwood Road
Kennett Square, PA 19348-1807
Tel: 610-708-3010
http://www.publicgardens.org

For information on student membership and certification, contact
Professional Grounds Management Society
720 Light Street
Baltimore, MD 21230-3850
Tel: 410-223-2861
E-mail: pgms@assnhqtrs.com
http://www.pgms.org

*For information on certification, careers, internships, and student
membership, contact*
Professional Landcare Network
950 Herndon Parkway, Suite 450
Herndon, VA 20170-5528
Tel: 800-395-2522
http://www.landcarenetwork.org

For information on the agricultural industry, contact
U.S. Department of Agriculture
1400 Independence Avenue, SW
Washington, DC 20250-0002
Tel: 202-720-2791
http://www.usda.gov

Organic Farmers

QUICK FACTS

School Subjects
Agriculture
Business
English
Mathematics

Personal Skills
Business/management
Communication/ideas

Work Environment
Indoors and outdoors
Primarily one location

Minimum Education Level
Associate's degree

Salary Range
$18,900 to $32,350 to
$91,710+

Certification or Licensing
May be required, depends on
size and scope of business

Outlook
About as fast as the average

DOT
040

GOE
03.01.01

NOC
8251

O*NET-SOC
11-9012.00

OVERVIEW

Organic farmers manage farms that produce fruits, vegetables, herbs, dairy, or other products without the use of inorganic fertilizers and synthetic chemical herbicides, growth hormones, and synthetic pesticides. Depending on the size of the farm, organic farmers manage staff; handle crop production and schedules; work the land; operate and maintain machinery, and repair farm structures; take care of administrative tasks such as bookkeeping, tax reporting, phone calls, and e-mails; and market and promote the farm business.

HISTORY

Organic farming is an ancient practice, dating back to early civilizations, and was the only form of agriculture for thousands of years. Its distinction as "organic" was not needed, nor made, until the early 20th century, when another type of agricultural practice emerged that relied on synthetic fertilizers and chemicals to improve and increase crop productions. Sir Albert Howard, a British agriculturist, is considered by many to be the father of organic farming. He studied agricultural practices in India from 1905 to 1934, and later wrote books, such as *An Agricultural Testament*, about composting and soil fertility, recycling organic waste materials for use in farming, and his adamant opposition to the use of chemical fertilizers in farming.

Chemicals that were developed for use in World War II were adapted, post-war, for use in crop production in the United States;

A customer talks with an organic farmer at a farmers' market. *(Clare Howard, AP Photo/Journal Star)*

for instance, nerve gases were used as strong pesticides. To combat mosquitoes and other pests, these chemicals were used widely on crops around the country. It wasn't until 1962, when ecologist Rachel Carson's book *Silent Spring* came out, that the general public became fully aware of what these chemicals were doing to the environment, to wildlife and ecosystems, and to human beings. From the book, people learned that DDT (dichlorodiphenyltrichloroethane), a colorless, chlorine-containing pesticide, was killing a number of different bird species (thus the book's title, silent spring), and that pesticides stay in people's systems their entire lives. Carson advocated for more responsible use of the chemicals, and for agricultural and chemical companies to be forthcoming about the use of these chemicals. DDT was banned in 1972, and *Silent Spring* is credited for kicking off the environmental movement.

Organic farming has evolved since the 1970s to take many forms. In the early days, many organic farmers started their businesses to directly counter large, industrialized farms. The small, independently operated organic farm still exists today, as do large, corporate farms. The term *organic* has evolved and been popularized, with people now interpreting it to mean anything from "free of chemicals" to "USDA organic certified." With "organic" becoming more closely associated with a corporate logo and large agribusiness, many small- and medium-sized organic farms are instead using the words *sustainable* and *natural* to describe their farming practices.

THE JOB

The International Federation of Organic Agriculture Movements defines organic farming as "a production system that sustains the health of soils, ecosystems, and people. It relies on ecological processes, biodiversity, and cycles adapted to local conditions, rather than the use of inputs with adverse effects. Organic agriculture combines tradition, innovation, and science to benefit the shared environment and promote fair relationships and a good quality of life for all involved."

Organic farmers either own the organic farmland on which they work, rent the land from the owner, or lease it through a land trust. Organic farmers may therefore be the farmland and business owners, *farm operators*, or they may be *farm managers*. They may come from a long line of farmers or they may be new to the business. On small farms, organic farmers have fewer staff and more diverse, wide-ranging responsibilities. They may be involved in more of the physical labor in addition to hiring and managing staff; researching, purchasing, and maintaining farm equipment; and researching and strategizing the types of crops to grow, the types of seeds to plant, and the timing of plantings and harvestings.

Some organic farmers change careers to become farmers, such as Keith Stewart. He was 40 when, in 1986, he traded in a well-established career as a project manager (and a tiny apartment) in New York City for an "unkempt but fully functional dairy farm" 70 miles north of the city, in Westtown, New York. The 88-acre site, known as Keith's Farm, that he and his then-girlfriend, now-wife Flavia Bacarella purchased, includes an old house and a barn, "woods and fields, ridges and vales, a pond and a stream," as well as chickens, dogs, cats, and plenty of wildlife. The organic farm started as a one-person operation and has since grown to include a rotating staff of six to eight workers per year. And while the work of being a farmer has been, and continues to be, hard, Keith still believes the challenges are well worth the toil. "There has been much to learn," he says. "But when your heart agrees with what you are doing, the learning is easier and more fun. I've done many other kinds of work in my life, but none where I felt as appreciated or needed." Keith's Farm has developed a loyal clientele since it first broke ground and is the "longest-standing purveyor" at the Union Square Greenmarket in New York City.

A big part of organic farming involves soil management through crop rotation (also known as crop sequencing). To keep the soil fertile and help control pests and diseases, organic farmers will use the same farmland to plant a different crop in a schedule of either successive seasons or every few years. Composting is also part of the job description. Compost, or "green manure," is a natural fertilizer that can be created by mixing such things as decaying vegetables and food wastes, paper and yard wastes (such as grass clippings), and animal waste (manure). Granted, it's not a pretty smell, but the combination is rich in minerals that help fertilize and condition the soil.

Depending on the size of the farm, organic farmers are responsible for preparing the land, mechanical tilling, weeding (by hand, tools, and devices such as the flame-weeder, which literally shoots flame to burn weeds), mulching, planting, fertilizing (composting), cultivating, and harvesting, and this is by no means an all-inclusive list. Work hours are especially long during planting, growing, and harvesting seasons. Once the harvest is over, they make sure that the produce is properly packaged, stored, and marketed. Many farmers participate in farmers' markets, and while this boosts sales, it also adds to the farmers' workload. It requires creating the vending booth (such as signage, product packaging, literature for takeaways, etc.); packing up and trucking the products to the market; setting up the booth; and either working at the market and interacting with consumers and handling transactions, or staffing the booth and managing the staffing schedules. And at the end of marketing day, every task needs to be reversed: The booth needs to be broken down, products must be packed up and brought back to the farm, and then the tallying and bookkeeping of the transactions can begin.

During cold seasons, farmers may plant cover crops, which are crops that are planted primarily to provide ground cover, prevent erosion, and improve soil properties. Cover crops may be wheat, oats, or rye, or can even be legumes, such as clover and alfalfa.

Organic farmers might also produce products such as milk, cheese, yogurt, and eggs. All organic dairy products and eggs must come from animals that are fed organic feed and are provided with access to open space where they can comfortably roam and enjoy the sunlight. Organic livestock and poultry may not be given antibiotics, hormones, or medications, but they may be vaccinated against disease.

REQUIREMENTS

High School

While in high school, take classes in business, math, earth science, ecology, agriculture (if offered), biology, English, and computers. Foreign language classes can also be useful, as can participation in 4-H or FFA programs.

Postsecondary Training

Self-employed farmers may have received their training while on the job, either from growing up in a farm family, or through adult on-the-job training and continuing education courses and programs in agriculture. Others may have an associate's or bachelor's degree in agriculture, which is becoming more important in the business of operating a farm. Degrees can be earned in farm management or in business with a concentration in agriculture. According to the U.S. Department of Labor (DOL), all state universities have a land-grant college or university with a school of agriculture. Students pursuing an agriculture degree typically take classes in agronomy, dairy science, agricultural economics and business, horticulture, crop and fruit science, and animal science. They may also study technical aspects of crops, growing conditions, and plant diseases. If interested in organic dairy farming, course work may include the basics of veterinary science and animal husbandry (which is the care and breeding of farm animals). Other key courses include climate change, the impact of farming on the environment, economic policy (as it relates to farming and farmland), as well as business management and accounting. Computer classes are also relevant as more farming businesses are using computer software programs for record keeping and document production. Many farms offer internships and apprenticeships, in which students can train while on the job, and earn school credit and possibly a small stipend in exchange for their work.

Certification or Licensing

Since 2002 the U.S. Department of Agriculture (USDA) National Organic Program (NOP) has regulated the standards for farms that want to sell organic products. Farms that produce less than $5,000 worth of organic products per year are not required by the USDA to be certified. To receive the organic certification and use the official "USDA Organic" label, at least 95 percent of the ingredients must be organic and meet the USDA standards for organic production and processes. For some farmers, especially those at beginning and small farms, the USDA certification process can be expensive, and financial assistance may be required. The certification process also requires evidence of an organic farming plan, paperwork to verify the plan, and a certain number of farm inspections. Third-party agents are hired to conduct the inspections of the farmer, the farm, the production process, as well as all who work on the farm.

Keith's Farm, for example, was originally certified by the North-east Organic Farming Association of New York (NOFA-NY), at a time when it set its own rules and standards for organic farming certification. The organization has since changed its name to NOFA-NY Certified Organic LLC, and is now following USDA national standards for organic certification.

According to the Organic Farming Research Foundation, in 1994 there were approximately 2,500 to 3,000 certified organic farmers in the United States. As of 2007, the number had jumped to 13,000 certified organic farmers, and certified organic farmland could be found in all 50 states.

Other Requirements

Self-motivated, disciplined, detail oriented, and patient are the all-important character traits needed in organic farming. The self-motivation and discipline are called upon on a daily basis, and are especially crucial to have in the beginning years of farming. Waiting for things to grow—both the produce and the business itself—is where patience comes into play. As organic farmer Keith Stewart puts it, "We see the fruits of our labor and the results of our neglect. We are on good terms with the natural world, or we should be, and we inhabit it in a practical, down-to-earth way."

A love of the land and strong desire to work with and get closer to nature are a given in this job. Attention to detail while simultaneously juggling multiple tasks is also important on many levels, from managing the crop production and the farm staff, to managing and promoting the business itself and the products. "Dawn to dusk" does not quite cover the hours required to complete the work; the time commitment goes far, far beyond this. Excellent hand-eye coordination is required, as is the ability to safely handle farm equipment one moment and manage farm animals the next. Physical fitness, stamina, and energy are required and tested constantly. The work is predominantly outdoors in any kind of weather—be it teeming rain, blazing sunshine, bone-shattering cold, or the three deadly H's (hazy, hot, and humid). A good attitude, strong constitution, and openness to continually learn are extremely helpful attributes to have in this job.

EXPLORING

Keep your eyes and ears open for the documentary film *The Greenhorns*, directed by Severine von Tscharner Fleming, of Smithereen Farm in Hudson River Valley, New York. The film features conversations with young farmers across the country—those who deliberately set out to become farmers, and those who "accidentally" fell into it. The film advocates for choosing agriculture as a career. You can learn more about *The Greenhorns* and find other resources, such as "The Greenhorns Guide for Beginning Farmers," by visiting the Web site (http://www.thegreenhorns.net).

Another excellent way to explore the field (without breaking a sweat) is by reading books such as Keith Stewart's *It's a Long Road to a Tomato: Tales of an Organic Farmer Who Quit the Big City for the (Not So) Simple Life,* 2nd edition (New York: Marlowe & Company, 2010); and Peter V. Fossel's *Organic Farming: Everything You Need to Know* (Osceola, Wis.: Voyageur Press, 2007). The trade publication *Farmers' Market Today* (http://www.farmersmarketsto-day.com/fmt) is another useful resource that will keep you up-to-date on tips, trends, and resources for farmers.

EMPLOYERS

Nearly 1.2 million farmers, ranchers, and agricultural managers worked in the United States in 2008, according to the DOL. Nearly 80 percent were self-employed farmers and ranchers, and the rest were agricultural managers. Most worked in the area of crop-production management, while others were responsible for managing livestock and dairy production. Some organic farmers work independently on small farms; others may work on large farms and may oversee many farm workers and staff.

STARTING OUT

Volunteering or working part time on an organic farm is an excellent way to learn what it takes to succeed in and enjoy being an organic farmer. A willingness to relocate to have the farm experience can also broaden the range of opportunities. For example, Qayyum Johnson had worked on a farm in California before moving to New York to work on Keith's Farm. And Matt Ready, an intern with

Keith's Farm since June 2009, found his internship through ATTRA, an organization that offers a national directory called "Sustainable Farming Internships and Apprenticeships." (You can find the directory at: http://attra.ncat.org/attra-pub/internships.) Matt had been studying computer science and doing landscaping work in Indiana when he got the idea about working on a farm. He started exploring farms around the country, and his sister's recent move to New York City inspired him to look closer at farms in the New York area. The internship at Keith's Farm was posted in ATTRA's directory. Matt and Qayyum live and work on the farm, along with a small team of workers. Their tasks are varied, including helping with plantings, harvestings, and greenhouse work; pitching in at the greenmarket; and tending to the chickens (and the eggs).

The nonprofit organization World-Wide Opportunities on Organic Farms (WWOOF) lists farms around the world where volunteers are needed. Visit the U.S. Web site to learn more about opportunities within the states (http://www.wwoofusa.org), or if you're more adventurous and able to travel and spend a summer, or longer, away from home, visit the WWOOF headquarters' Web site (http://www.wwoof.org/index.asp).

ADVANCEMENT

The path of advancement in the farming business depends on the farmer. For some, advancement can come in the form of expanding into different products (such as offering baked goods in addition to produce), or increasing the size of the farm and the crops, and adding more staff. Advancement can also include participating in more farmers' markets, or starting up a community-supported aspect of the farm. For other farmers, advancement may take a more meditative, educational path, one that might lead to writing books and articles, or teaching, lecturing, and mentoring young farmers and students. Some even start restaurants on or near the farm.

EARNINGS

Annual salaries for organic farmers vary each year, depending on the quantity and quality of the farm's products and consumers' demands for those products. Small farms that are new may not see much, if any, profit during the first few years of the business. And even farms that have been in business for many years, with a longstanding customer base, may see large profit one year and less profit the following year.

The DOL reports that in 2009, farmers and ranchers earned median annual incomes of $32,350, with the lowest paid 10 percent bringing home $18,900 or less per year, and the top paid 10 percent earning $91,710 or more annually. According to the USDA, in 2007 established farms had annual household incomes in the $90,866 range. Beginning farmers had household incomes that were 4 percent lower than those of established farm households. (The USDA defines "beginning farm" as one that's been in operation for less than 10 years.) According to an article in the USDA's publication *Amber Waves*, farmers work well past retirement, and tend to have "several income sources, different savings habits, and more diverse financial portfolios, including more personal savings, than other U.S. households." Farmers often supplement their incomes by working in other jobs as well, which can include running a separate business, teaching, or writing.

WORK ENVIRONMENT

Farmers work from dawn to dusk, rain or shine, and will work even longer hours during plantings and harvestings. If they run a small farm with few staff members, more of the responsibilities will fall to them, making for longer days and little, if any, time off. Much of their day is spent outside working the land, but they also spend some time indoors addressing the administrative side of the business, which can include conducting Internet research and reviewing and paying bills, among other tasks. They may spend some time traveling to participate in farmers' markets, conferences, and workshops.

OUTLOOK

The industrialization of agriculture has enabled large-scale farming businesses to get more done with fewer workers. This coupled with a continuing population growth and consequential urban sprawl (the spread of development, such as houses and shopping centers, into nearby undeveloped land, often prime farmland)—plus surging costs of land, machinery, and other farming necessities—has caused the demise of many farms, and made it especially challenging for young and beginning farmers to start their farming business. Larger, better-funded, and more established farms have been able to withstand the pressures, as well as take advantage of government subsidies and payments, since these are typically based on the amount of acreage owned and the per-unit production.

While the DOL forecasts a decline in employment (by about 8 percent) of self-employed farmers and ranchers through 2018, farmers who run small- and medium-sized businesses in a specific niche can take heart that they will find more opportunities in the industry. Organic farmers who cater to urban and suburban customers, particularly by participating in farmers' markets and community-supported programs and cooperatives, will find that they have more avenues in which to promote their farms and sell their products. To further bolster this, reports show that more farmers' markets are opening every year in cities and suburbs throughout the country. In 1994 there were 1,755 farmers' markets operating in the United States; by 2009 that number had grown to 5,274, according to the USDA's Agricultural Marketing Service.

FOR MORE INFORMATION

Learn more about sustainable food and farm systems, and steps being taken to protect land and keep it healthy by visiting
American Farmland Trust
1200 18th Street, NW, Suite 800
Washington, DC 20036-2524
Tel: 202-331-7300
E-mail: info@farmland.org
http://www.farmland.org

Learn more about organic and sustainable farming and the certification program at the NOFA-NY Certified Organic LLC Web site.
NOFA-NY Certified Organic LLC
840 Upper Front Street
Binghamton, NY 13905-1566
Tel: 607-724-9851
E-mail: certifiedorganic@nofany.org
https://www.nofany.org

Find organic farming research and learn more about issues related to the industry by visiting
Organic Farming Research Foundation
PO Box 440
Santa Cruz, CA 95061-0440
Tel: 831-426-6606
E-mail: info@ofrf.org
http://ofrf.org

Find membership information, books, public policy updates, and other resources on the OTA Web site.
Organic Trade Association (OTA)
28 Vernon Street, Suite 413
Brattleboro, VT 05301-3674
Tel: 802-275-3800
http://www.ota.com

Find resources and events for small farms and beginning farmers by visiting
U.S. Department of Agriculture
National Institute of Food and Agriculture
1400 Independence Avenue, SW, Stop 2201
Washington, DC 20250-2201
Tel: 202-720-4423
http://www.csrees.usda.gov/familysmallfarms.cfm

This organization is "part of a worldwide effort to link volunteers with organic farmers, promote an educational exchange, and build a global community conscious of ecological farming practices." Visit its U.S. Web site to learn more about volunteer opportunities on organic farms located across the country.
World-Wide Opportunities on Organic Farms-USA
430 Forest Avenue
Laguna Beach, CA 92651-2331
Tel: 949-715-9500
E-mail: info@wwoofusa.org
http://www.wwoofusa.org

Range Managers

OVERVIEW

Range managers maintain and improve grazing lands on public and private property. They research, develop, and carry out methods to improve and increase the production of forage plants, livestock, and wildlife without damaging the environment; develop and carry out plans for water facilities, erosion control, and soil treatments; restore rangelands that have been damaged by fire, pests, and undesirable plants; and manage the upkeep of range improvements, such as fences, corrals, and reservoirs. Range managers are sometimes known as *range scientists, range ecologists, rangeland management specialists,* and *range conservationists.*

HISTORY

Early in history, primitive peoples grazed their livestock wherever forage was plentiful. As the supply of grass and shrubs became depleted, they simply moved on, leaving the stripped land to suffer the effects of soil erosion. When civilization grew and the nomadic tribes began to establish settlements, people began to recognize the need for conservation and developed simple methods of land terracing, irrigation, and the rotation of grazing lands.

Much the same thing happened in the United States. The rapid expansion across the continent in the 19th century was accompanied by the destruction of plant and animal life and the abuse of the soil. Because the country's natural resources appeared inexhaustible, the cries of alarm that came from a few concerned conservationists went unheeded. It was not until after 1890 that conservation became a national policy. Today several state and federal agencies are actively involved in protecting the nation's soil, water, forests, and wildlife.

QUICK FACTS

School Subjects
Biology
Earth science

Personal Skills
Leadership/management
Technical/scientific

Work Environment
Indoors and outdoors
Primarily multiple locations

Minimum Education Level
Bachelor's degree

Salary Range
$35,570 to $64,564 to $87,890+

Certification or Licensing
Voluntary

Outlook
About as fast as the average

DOT
040

GOE
02.03.02

NOC
2223

O*NET-SOC
19-1031.02

Rangelands cover more than a billion acres of the United States, mostly in the western states and Alaska. Many natural resources are found there: grass and shrubs for animal grazing, wildlife habitats, water from vast watersheds, recreation facilities, and valuable mineral and energy resources. In addition, rangelands are used by scientists who conduct studies of the environment.

THE JOB

Range managers seek to maximize range resources without damaging the environment. They accomplish this in a number of ways.

To help ranchers attain optimum production of livestock, range managers study the rangelands to determine the number and kind of livestock that can be most profitably grazed, the grazing system to use, and the best seasons for grazing. The system they recommend must be designed to conserve the soil and vegetation for other uses, such as wildlife habitats, outdoor recreation, and timber.

Grazing lands must continually be restored and improved. Range managers study plants to determine which varieties are best suited to a particular range and to develop improved methods for reseeding. They devise biological, chemical, or mechanical ways of controlling undesirable and poisonous plants, and they design methods of protecting the range from grazing damage.

Range managers also develop and help carry out plans for water facilities, structures for erosion control, and soil treatments. They are responsible for the construction and maintenance of such improvements as fencing, corrals, and reservoirs for stock watering.

Although range managers spend a great deal of time outdoors, they also work in offices, consulting with other conservation specialists, preparing written reports, and doing administrative work.

Rangelands have more than one use, so range managers often work in such closely related fields as wildlife and watershed management, forest management, and recreation. *Soil conservationists* and *naturalists* are concerned with maintaining ecological balance both on the range and in forest preserves.

REQUIREMENTS

High School

If you are interested in pursuing a career in range management, you should begin planning your education early. Since you will need a college degree for this work, take college preparatory classes in high school. Your class schedule should include the sciences, such as earth science, biology, and chemistry. Take mathematics and economics

Range managers review a range management plan. *(Ron Nichols, Natural Resources Conservation Service)*

classes. Any courses that teach you to use a computer will also be beneficial. You will frequently use this tool in your career to keep records, file reports, and do planning. English courses will also help you develop your research, writing, and reading skills. You will need all of these skills in college and beyond.

Postsecondary Training

The minimum educational requirement for range managers is usually a bachelor's degree in range management or range science. To be hired by the federal government, you will need at least 42 credit hours in plant, animal, or soil sciences and natural resources management courses, including at least 18 hours in range management. If you would like a teaching or research position, you will need a graduate degree in range management. Advanced degrees may also prove helpful for advancement in other jobs.

To receive a bachelor's degree in range management, students must have acquired a basic knowledge of biology, chemistry, physics, mathematics, and communication skills. Specialized courses in range management combine plant, animal, and soil sciences with the principles of ecology and resource management. Students are also encouraged to take electives, such as economics, forestry, hydrology, agronomy, wildlife, and computer science.

While a number of schools offer some courses related to range management, only nine colleges and universities have degree programs in range management or range science that are accredited by the Society for Range Management. More than 40 other schools offer course work available in a discipline with a range management or range science option.

Certification or Licensing
The Society for Range Management offers the certified range management consultant and certified professional in rangeland management designations. These are voluntary certifications, but earning them demonstrates a professional's commitment to the field and the high quality of his or her work. Requirements for certification include having a bachelor's degree and at least five years of experience in the field as well as passing a written exam.

Other Requirements
Along with their technical skills, range managers must be able to speak and write effectively and to work well with others. Range managers need to be self-motivated and flexible. They are generally persons who do not want the restrictions of an office setting and a rigid schedule. They should have a love for the outdoors as well as good health and physical stamina for the strenuous activity that this occupation requires.

EXPLORING
As a high school student, you can test your appetite for outdoor work by applying for summer jobs on ranches or farms. Other ways of exploring this occupation include a field trip to a ranch or interviews with or lectures by range managers, ranchers, or conservationists. Any volunteer work with conservation organizations—large or small—will give you an idea of what range managers do and will help you when you apply to colleges and for employment.

As a college student, you can get more direct experience by applying for summer jobs in range management with such federal agencies as the Forest Service, the Natural Resources Conservation Service (NRCS), and the Bureau of Land Management (BLM). This experience may better qualify you for jobs when you graduate.

EMPLOYERS
The majority of range managers are employed by the federal government in the Forest Service and NRCS (both part of the U.S.

Department of Agriculture) or the BLM (part of the U.S. Department of the Interior). State governments employ range managers in game and fish departments, state land agencies, and extension services. A small percentage are self-employed.

In private industry, the number of range managers is increasing. They work for coal and oil companies to help reclaim mined areas, for banks and real estate firms to help increase the revenue from landholdings, and for private consulting firms, nonprofit organizations, and large ranches. Some range managers with advanced degrees teach and do research at colleges and universities. Others work overseas with U.S. and United Nations agencies and with foreign governments.

STARTING OUT

The usual way to enter this occupation is to apply directly to the appropriate government agencies. People interested in working for the federal government may contact the Forest Service or the NRCS, or the Department of the Interior's Bureau of Indian Affairs or the BLM. Others may apply to local state employment offices for jobs in state land agencies, game and fish departments, or agricultural extension services. Your college career services office should have listings of available jobs.

ADVANCEMENT

Range managers may advance to administrative positions in which they plan and supervise the work of others and write reports. Others may go into teaching or research. An advanced degree is often necessary for the higher level jobs in this field. Another way for range managers to advance is to enter business for themselves as range management consultants or ranchers.

EARNINGS

The average federal salary for rangeland managers was $64,564 in 2009, according to the U.S. Department of Labor (DOL). Salaries for conservation scientists ranged from less than $35,570 to $87,890 or more.

State governments and private companies pay their range managers salaries that are about the same as those paid by the federal government. Range managers are also eligible for paid vacations and sick days, health and life insurance, and other benefits.

WORK ENVIRONMENT

Range managers, particularly those just beginning their careers, spend a great deal of time on the range. That means they must work outdoors in all kinds of weather. They usually travel by car or small plane, but in rough country they use four-wheel-drive vehicles or get around on horseback or on foot. When riding the range, managers may spend a considerable amount of time away from home, and the work is often quite strenuous.

As range managers advance to administrative jobs, they spend more time working in offices, writing reports, and planning and supervising the work of others. Range managers may work alone or under direct supervision; often they work as part of a team. In any case, they must deal constantly with people—not only their superiors and coworkers but with the general public, ranchers, government officials, and other conservation specialists.

OUTLOOK

The DOL predicts that employment for conservation scientists and foresters, a category that includes range managers, will grow about as fast as the average for all occupations through 2018. This is a small occupation, and most of the openings will arise when older, experienced range managers retire or leave the occupation. The need for range managers should be stimulated by a growing demand for wildlife habitats, recreation, and water as well as by an increasing concern for the environment. A greater number of large ranches will employ range managers to improve range management practices and increase output and profitability. Range specialists will also be employed in larger numbers by private industry to reclaim lands damaged by oil and coal exploration. A small number of new jobs will result from the need for range and soil conservationists to provide technical assistance to owners of grazing land through the NRCS.

An additional demand for range managers could be created by the conversion of rangelands to other purposes, such as wildlife habitats and recreation. Federal employment for these activities, however, depends on the passage of legislation concerning the management of range resources, an area that is always controversial. Smaller budgets may also limit employment growth in this area.

FOR MORE INFORMATION

For information about career opportunities in the federal government, contact

Bureau of Indian Affairs
U.S. Department of the Interior
1849 C Street, NW
MS-3658-MIB
Washington, DC 20240-0001
Tel: 202-208-3710
http://www.bia.gov

Bureau of Land Management
U.S. Department of the Interior
1849 C Street, Room 5665
Washington, DC 20240-0001
http://www.blm.gov

National Park Service
U.S. Department of the Interior
1849 C Street, NW
Washington, DC 20240-0001
Tel: 202-208-6843
http://www.nps.gov

Natural Resources Conservation Service
U.S. Department of Agriculture
1400 Independence Avenue, SW
Washington, DC 20250-0002
http://www.nrcs.usda.gov

U.S. Forest Service
U.S. Department of Agriculture
1400 Independence Avenue, SW
Washington, DC 20250-0003
Tel: 800-832-1355
http://www.fs.fed.us

Career and education information may be obtained from
National Recreation and Park Association
22377 Belmont Ridge Road
Ashburn, VA 20148-4501
Tel: 800-626-6772
http://www.nrpa.org

This organization has career, education, scholarship, and certifica-
tion information. Student membership is also available through its
International Student Conclave.

Society for Range Management
10030 West 27th Avenue
Wheat Ridge, CO 80215-6601
Tel: 303-986-3309
E-mail: info@rangelands.org
http://www.rangelands.org

INTERVIEW

Richard Mayberry is a rangeland management specialist who is employed by the Bureau of Land Management (BLM), an agency of the U.S. Department of the Interior. He discussed his career with the editors of Careers in Focus: Agriculture.

Q. How long have you worked in the field?

A. I have been employed by the BLM since 1977, and have worked in southern Idaho, southeastern Oregon, and in Washington D.C. The BLM manages 252 million acres of public land for multiple uses, mostly in the western states and Alaska. The BLM also manages about 700 million acres of minerals, some of which are located under private lands, tribal lands, and other public lands managed by other federal agencies.

Q. Why did you decide to enter this career?

A. When I was a high school student in eastern Washington State, I wanted to be a forester, but my counselor thought that I would be at a disadvantage in college because I lived on the desert side of the state rather than the forested side. He convinced me I would not compete well with the students who had grown up on the forested side of the state and suggested I should consider range management. After receiving my degree in range conservation, I began working for the BLM as a range conservationist. My major responsibilities were gathering and interpreting vegetation and soils data, and working with ranchers to develop grazing plans to maintain good conditions for forage production, wildlife habitat, and clean water. My current responsibilities in the BLM headquarters office are to develop policy, assist field offices with technical information, coordinate with other agencies, and provide information to Congress. I supervised other BLM staff specialists for 12 years in Idaho and Oregon.

　　The main reason I chose a career in natural resource management was because I wanted to spend time outdoors and be part of maintaining or achieving good conditions on public lands in the west.

Q. What do you like most and least about your job?

A. What I like best about the work I have done in the last 33 years is the opportunity to work with other BLM employees, ranchers, and environmental organizations [that] want to work together to improve public land conditions. What I find most challenging is working with people and organizations that want to improve public land conditions but are unwilling to work with others.

Q. What is the future employment outlook for range managers?

A. There is and will continue to be good opportunity for employment as a range specialist or natural resource specialist with the BLM. High school students would benefit from being active in clubs or classes that develop communication skills, including speaking and writing, and those that give opportunity to explore their level of interest in natural resources management. These could include classes in public speaking, biology/botany, and physical sciences. Membership in National FFA Organization, the Society for Range Management, and community volunteer organizations will help students develop both technical skills and an understanding of how to work cooperatively with others.

Soil Conservationists and Soil Conservation Technicians

OVERVIEW

Soil conservationists develop conservation plans to help farmers and ranchers, developers, homeowners, and government officials best use their land while adhering to government conservation regulations. They suggest plans to conserve and reclaim soil, preserve or restore wetlands and other rare ecological areas, rotate crops for increased yields and soil conservation, reduce water pollution, and restore or increase wildlife populations. They assess land users' needs, costs, maintenance requirements, and the life expectancy of various conservation practices. They plan design specifications using survey and field information, technical guides, and engineering field manuals. Soil conservationists also give talks to various organizations to educate land users and the public about how to conserve and restore soil and water resources. Many of their recommendations are based on information provided to them by soil scientists.

Soil conservation technicians work more directly with land users by putting the ideas and plans of the conservationist into action. In their work they use basic engineering and surveying tools, instruments, and techniques. They perform engineering surveys and design and implement conservation practices like terraces and grassed waterways. Soil conservation technicians monitor projects during and after construction and periodically revisit the site to evaluate the practices and plans.

HISTORY

In 1908, President Theodore Roosevelt appointed a National Conservation Commission to oversee the proper conservation of the country's natural resources. As a result, many state and local conservation organizations were formed, and Americans began to take a serious interest in preserving their land's natural resources.

QUICK FACTS

(continued)

NOC
2123

O*NET-SOC
19-1031.00, 19-4093.00,
45-4011.00

Despite this interest, however, conservation methods were not always understood or implemented. For example, farmers in the southern Great Plains, wanting to harvest a cash crop, planted many thousands of acres of wheat during the early decades of the 20th century. The crop was repeated year after year until the natural grasslands of the area were destroyed and the soil was depleted of nutrients. When the area experienced prolonged droughts combined with the naturally occurring high winds, devastating dust storms swept the land during the 1930s. Parts of Oklahoma, Texas, Kansas, New Mexico, and Colorado suffered from severe soil erosion that resulted in desert-like conditions, and this ruined area became known as the Dust Bowl.

As a result of what happened to the Dust Bowl, Congress established the Natural Resources Conservation Service of the U.S. Department of Agriculture in 1935. Because more than 800 million tons of topsoil had already been blown away by the winds over the plains, the job of reclaiming the land through wise conservation practices was not an easy one. In addition to the large areas of the Great Plains that had become desert land, there were other badly eroded lands throughout the country.

Fortunately, emergency planning came to the aid of the newly established conservation program. The Civilian Conservation Corps (CCC) was created to help alleviate unemployment during the Great Depression of the 1930s. The CCC established camps in rural areas and assigned people to aid in many different kinds of conservation. Soil conservationists directed those portions of the CCC program designed to halt the loss of topsoil by wind and water action.

Much progress has been made in the years since the Natural Resource Conservation Service was established. Wasted land has

Words to Know

Aeration porosity: The fraction of the volume of soil that is filled with air at any given time.

Gytta: Peat consisting of plant and animal residues from standing water.

Karst: Topography with caves, sinkholes, and underground drainage that is formed in limestone and other rocks by dissolution.

Macronutrient: A nutrient found in high concentrations in a plant.

Scarp: A cliff or steep slope along the margin of a plateau.

been reclaimed and further loss has been prevented. Land-grant colleges have initiated programs to help farmers understand the principles and procedures of soil conservation. The National Institute of Food and Agriculture (within the Department of Agriculture) provides workers who are skilled in soil conservation to work with these programs.

Throughout the United States today there are several thousand federally appointed soil conservation districts. A worker employed by the government works in these districts to demonstrate soil conservation to farmers and agricultural businesses. There are usually one or more professional soil conservationists and one or more soil conservation technicians working in each district.

THE JOB

Soil sustains plant and animal life, influences water and air quality, and supports human health and habitation. Its quality has a major impact on ecological balance, biological diversity, air quality, water flow, and plant growth, including crops and forestation. Soil conservationists and technicians help scientists and engineers collect samples and data to determine soil quality, identify problems, and develop plans to better manage the land. They work with farmers, agricultural professionals, landowners, range managers, and public and private agencies to establish and maintain sound conservation practices.

A farmer or landowner contacts soil conservationists to help identify soil quality problems, improve soil quality, maintain it, or stop or reverse soil degradation. Conservationists visit the site to gather information, beginning with past and current uses of the soil and future plans for the site. They consult precipitation and soil maps and try to determine if the way land is being currently used is somehow degrading the soil quality. Conservationists consider irrigation practices, fertilizer use, and tillage systems. At least a five- to 10-year history of land use is most helpful for working in this field.

Site observation reveals signs of soil quality problems. The farmer or landowner can point out areas of concern that occur regularly, such as wet spots, salt accumulation, rills and gullies, or excessive runoff water that could indicate erosion, stunted plant growth, or low crop yield. Samples are taken from these areas and tested for such physical, chemical, and biological properties as soil fertility, soil structure, soil stability, water storage and availability, and nutrient retention. Conservationists also look at plant characteristics, such as rooting depth, which can indicate density or compaction of the soil.

Once all the data are gathered and samples tested, conservationists analyze the results. They look for patterns and trends. If necessary, they take additional samples to verify discrepancies or confirm results. They prepare a report for the farmer or landowner.

A team of conservationists, engineers, scientists, and the landowners propose alternative solutions for soil problems. All the alternatives must be weighed carefully for their possible effects on ecological balance, natural resources, economic factors, and social or cultural factors. The landowner makes the final decision on which solutions to use and a plan is drafted.

After the plan is in place, soil conservationists and technicians continue to monitor and evaluate soil conditions, usually over a period of several years. Periodic soil sampling shows whether progress is being made, and if not, changes can be made to the plan.

These brief examples show how the process works. A farmer has a problem with crop disease. He sees that the yield is reduced and the health of plants is poor. Soil conservationists and technicians consider possible causes and test soil for pests, nutrient deficiencies, lack of biological diversity, saturated soil, and compacted layers. Depending on test results, conservationists might suggest a pest-management program, an improved drainage system, the use of animal manure, or crop rotation.

Another farmer notices the formation of rills and gullies on his land along with a thinning topsoil layer. Soil conservationists' research shows that the erosion is due to such factors as lack of cover, excessive tillage that moves soil down a slope, intensive crop rotation, and low organic matter. Suggested solutions include reducing tillage, using animal manure, planting cover crops or strip crops, and using windbreaks.

Conservationists and technicians who work for the Bureau of Land Management, which oversees hundreds of millions of acres of public domain land, help survey publicly owned areas and pinpoint land features to determine the best use of public lands. Soil conservation technicians in the Bureau of Reclamation assist civil, construction, materials, or general engineers. Their job is to oversee certain phases of such projects as the construction of dams and irrigation planning. The bureau's ultimate goal is the control of water and soil resources for the benefit of farms, homes, and cities.

Other soil conservationists and technicians work as *range managers* and *technicians*, who help determine the value of rangeland, its grazing capabilities, erosion hazards, and livestock potential. (See Range Managers for more information.) *Physical science technicians* gather data in the field, studying the physical characteristics of the soil, make routine chemical analyses, and set up and operate test apparatus. *Cartographic survey technicians* work with *cartographers* (mapmakers) to map or chart the earth or graphically represent geographical information, survey the public domain, set boundaries, pinpoint land features, and determine the most beneficial public use. *Engineering technicians* conduct field tests and oversee some phases of construction on dams and irrigation projects. They also measure acreage, place property boundaries, and define drainage areas on maps. *Surveying technicians* perform surveys for field measurement and mapping, to plan for construction, to check the accuracy of dredging operations, or to provide reference points and lines for related work. They gather data for the design and construction of highways, dams, topographic maps, and nautical or aeronautical charts.

REQUIREMENTS

High School

While in high school, you should take at least one year each of algebra, geometry, and trigonometry. Take several years of English to develop your writing, research, and speaking skills as these are skills you will need when compiling reports and working with others. Science classes, of course, are important to take, including earth science, biology, and chemistry. If your high school offers agriculture classes, be sure to take any relating to land use, crop production, and soils.

Postsecondary Training

Conservationists hold bachelor's degrees in areas such as general agriculture, range management, crop or soil science, forestry, and agricultural engineering. Teaching and research positions require further graduate-level education in a natural resources field. Technicians typically have associate's degrees in one or more of the aforementioned majors. Though government jobs do not necessarily require a college degree (a combination of appropriate experience and education can serve as substitute), a college education can make you more desirable for a position.

Typical beginning courses include applied mathematics, basic soils, botany, chemistry, zoology, and introduction to range management. Advanced courses include American government, surveying, forestry, game management, soil and water conservation, economics, fish management, and conservation engineering.

Conservationists and technicians must have some practical experience in the use of soil conservation techniques before they enter the field. Many schools require students to work in the field during the school year or during summer vacation before they can be awarded their degree. Jobs are available in the federal park systems and with privately owned businesses.

Certification or Licensing

No certification or license is required of soil conservationists and technicians; however, becoming certified can improve your skills and professional standing. The American Society of Agronomy offers voluntary certification in soil science/classification.

Most government agencies require applicants to take a competitive examination for consideration.

Other Requirements

Soil conservationists and technicians must be able to apply practical as well as theoretical knowledge to their work. You must have a working knowledge of soil and water characteristics; be skilled in management of woodlands, wildlife areas, and recreation areas; and have knowledge of surveying instruments and practices, mapping, and the procedures used for interpreting aerial photographs.

Soil conservationists and technicians should also be able to write clear, concise reports to demonstrate and explain the results of tests, studies, and recommendations. A love for the outdoors and an appreciation for all natural resources are essential for success and personal fulfillment in this job.

EXPLORING

One of the best ways to become acquainted with soil conservation work and technology is through summer or part-time work on a farm or at a natural park. Other ways to explore this career include joining a local chapter of the 4-H Club or National FFA Organization (formerly Future Farmers of America). Science courses that include lab sections and mathematics courses focusing on practical problem solving will also help give you a feel for this kind of work.

EMPLOYERS

Nearly two-thirds of all conservation workers are employed by local and federal government agencies. At the federal level, most soil conservationists and technicians work for the Natural Resources Conservation Service, the Bureau of Land Management, and the Bureau of Reclamation. Others work for agencies at the state and county level. Soil conservationists and technicians also work for private agencies and firms such as banks and loan agencies, mining or steel companies, and public utilities. A small percentage of workers are self-employed consultants who advise private industry owners and government agencies.

STARTING OUT

Most students gain outside experience by working a summer job in their area of interest. You can get information on summer positions through your school's career services office. Often, contacts made on summer jobs lead to permanent employment after graduation. College career counselors and faculty members are often valuable sources of advice and information on finding employment.

Most soil conservationists and technicians find work with state, county, or federal agencies. Hiring procedures for these jobs vary according to the level of government in which the applicant is seeking work. In general, however, students begin the application procedure during the fourth semester of their program and take some form of competitive examination as part of the process. College career services personnel can help students find out about the application procedures. Representatives of government agencies often visit college campuses to explain employment opportunities to students and sometimes to recruit for their agencies.

ADVANCEMENT

Soil conservationists and technicians usually start out with a local conservation district to gain experience and expertise before advancing to the state, regional, or national level.

In many cases, conservationists and technicians continue their education while working by taking evening courses at a local college or technical institute. Federal agencies that employ conservationists and technicians have a policy of promotion from within. Because of this policy, there is a continuing opportunity for such workers to advance through the ranks. The degree of advancement that all conservationists and technicians can expect in their working careers is determined by their aptitudes, abilities, and, of course, their desire to advance.

Workers seeking a more dramatic change can transfer their skills to related jobs outside the conservation industry, such as farming or land appraisal.

EARNINGS

The majority of soil conservationists and technicians work for the federal government, and their salaries are determined by their government service rating. In 2009, the average annual salary for soil conservationists employed by the federal government was $69,483, according to the *Occupational Outlook Handbook*.

The U.S. Department of Labor (DOL) reports that median earnings for soil and plant scientists were $59,180 in 2009. Some scientists earned less than $34,930, while others earned $107,670 or more annually.

The DOL reports that median earnings for forest and conservation technicians (including those who specialize in soil science) were $32,860 in 2009. Salaries ranged from less than $24,490 to more than $53,080.

The salaries of conservationists and technicians working for private firms or agencies are roughly comparable to those paid by the federal government. Earnings at the state and local levels vary depending on the region but are typically lower.

Government jobs and larger private industries offer comprehensive benefit packages that are usually more generous than those offered by smaller firms.

WORK ENVIRONMENT

Soil conservationists and technicians usually work 40 hours per week except in unusual or emergency situations. They have opportunities to travel, especially when they work for federal agencies.

Soil conservation is an outdoor job. Workers travel to work sites by car but must often walk great distances to an assigned area. Although they sometimes work from aerial photographs and other on-site pictures, they cannot work from pictures alone. They must visit the spot that presents the problem in order to make appropriate recommendations.

Although soil conservationists and technicians spend much of their working time outdoors, indoor work is also necessary when generating detailed reports of their work to agency offices.

In their role as assistants to professionals, soil conservation technicians often assume the role of government public relations representatives when dealing with landowners and land managers. They must be able to explain the underlying principles of the structures that they design and the surveys that they perform.

To meet these and other requirements of the job, conservationists and technicians should be prepared to continue their education both formally and informally throughout their careers. They must stay aware of current periodicals and studies so that they can keep up-to-date in their areas of specialization.

Soil conservationists and technicians gain satisfaction from knowing that their work is vitally important to the nation's economy and environment. Without their expertise, large portions of land in the United States could become barren within a generation.

OUTLOOK

The DOL predicts that employment for conservation scientists (a category that includes soil conservationists) will grow about as fast as the average for all occupations through 2018, mainly due to an expected wave of retirement at state and federal agencies. The need for government involvement in protecting natural resources should remain strong. More opportunities may be available with state and local government agencies, which are aware of needs in their areas. The vast majority of America's cropland has suffered from some sort of erosion, and only continued efforts by soil conservation professionals can prevent a dangerous depletion of our most valuable resource: fertile soil.

Some soil conservationists and technicians are employed as research and testing experts for public utility companies, banks and loan agencies, and mining or steel companies. At present, a relatively small number of soil conservation workers are employed by these firms or agencies. However, these private-sector areas will provide an increasing number of employment opportunities over the next 10 years.

FOR MORE INFORMATION

For information on soil conservation careers and certification, contact

American Society of Agronomy
5585 Guilford Road
Madison, WI 53711-5801
Tel: 608-273-8080
https://www.agronomy.org

For information on seminars, issues affecting soil scientists, and educational institutions offering soil science programs, contact
National Society of Consulting Soil Scientists
PO Box 1219
Sandpoint, ID 83864-0860
Tel: 800-535-7148
http://www.nscss.org

Contact the NRCS for information on government soil conservation careers. Its Web site has information on volunteer opportunities.
Natural Resources Conservation Service (NRCS)
U.S. Department of Agriculture
1400 Independence Avenue, SW
Washington, DC 20250-0002
http://www.nrcs.usda.gov

For information on soil conservation, college student chapters, and publications, contact
Soil and Water Conservation Society
945 SW Ankeny Road
Ankeny, IA 50023-9723
Tel: 515-289-2331
http://www.swcs.org

For the career brochure Soils Sustain Life, *contact*
Soil Science Society of America
5585 Guilford Road
Madison, WI 53711-5801
Tel: 608-273-8080
https://www.soils.org

Soil Scientists

OVERVIEW

Soil scientists study the physical, chemical, and biological characteristics of soils to determine the most productive and effective planting strategies. Their research aids in producing larger, healthier crops and more environmentally sound farming procedures. There are approximately 14,000 soil and plant scientists in the United States.

HISTORY

Hundreds of years ago, farmers planted crops without restriction; they were unaware that soil could be depleted of necessary nutrients by overuse. When crops were poor, farmers often blamed the weather instead of their farming techniques.

Soil, one of our most important natural resources, was taken for granted until its condition became too bad to ignore. An increasing population, moreover, made the United States aware that its own welfare depends on fertile soil capable of producing food for hundreds of millions of people.

Increasing concerns about feeding a growing nation brought agricultural practices into reevaluation. In 1862, the U.S. Department of Agriculture (USDA) was created to give farmers information about new crops and improved farming techniques. Although the department started small, today the USDA is one of the largest agencies of the federal government.

Following the creation of the USDA, laws were created to further promote and protect farmers. The 1933 Agricultural Adjustment Act inaugurated a policy of giving direct government aid to farmers. Two years later, the Natural Resources Conservation Service was created after disastrous dust storms blew away millions of tons of valuable topsoil and destroyed fertile cropland throughout parts of Oklahoma, Texas, Kansas, New Mexico, and Colorado.

A soil scientist *(left)* shows a graduate student how to code and log soil samples. *(Peggy Greb, USDA, Agricultural Research Service)*

Since 1937, states have organized themselves into soil conservation districts. Each local division coordinates with the USDA, assigning soil scientists and soil conservationists to help local farmers establish and maintain farming practices that will use land in the wisest possible ways.

THE JOB

Soil is formed by the breaking of rocks and the decay of trees, plants, and animals. It may take as long as 500 years to make just one inch of topsoil. Unwise and wasteful farming methods can destroy that inch of soil in just a few short years. In addition, rainstorms may carry thousands of pounds of precious topsoil away and dissolve chemicals that are necessary to grow healthy crops through a process called erosion. Soil scientists work with engineers to address these issues.

Soil scientists spend much of their time outdoors, investigating fields, advising farmers about crop rotation or fertilizers, assessing field drainage, and taking soil samples. After researching an area, they may suggest certain crops to farmers to protect bare earth from the ravages of the wind and weather.

Soil scientists may also specialize in one particular aspect of the work. For example, they may work as a *soil mapper* or *soil surveyor*. These specialists study soil structure, origins, and capabilities through field observations, laboratory examinations, and controlled experimentation. Their investigations are aimed at determining the most suitable uses for a particular soil.

Soil fertility experts develop practices that will increase or maintain crop size. They must consider both the type of soil and the crop planted in their analysis. Various soils react differently when exposed to fertilizers, soil additives, crop rotation, and other farming techniques.

All soil scientists work in the laboratory. They examine soil samples under the microscope to determine bacterial and plant-food components. They also write reports based on their field notes and analyses done within the lab.

Soil science is part of the science of agronomy, which encompasses crop science. Soil and crop scientists work together in agricultural experiment stations during all seasons, doing research on crop production, soil fertility, and various kinds of soil management.

Some soil and crop scientists travel to remote sections of the world in search of plants and grasses that may thrive in this country and contribute to our food supply, pasture land, or soil replenishing efforts. Some scientists go overseas to advise farmers in other countries on how to treat their soils. Those with advanced degrees can teach college agriculture courses and conduct research projects.

REQUIREMENTS

High School

If you're interested in pursuing a career in agronomy, you should take college preparatory courses covering subjects such as math, science, English, and public speaking. Science courses, such as earth science, biology, and chemistry, are particularly important. Since much of your future work will involve calculations, you should take four years of high school math. You can learn a lot about farming methods and conditions by taking agriculture classes if your high school offers them. Computer science courses are also a good choice to familiarize yourself with this technology. You should also take English and speech courses, since soil scientists must write reports and make presentations about their findings.

Postsecondary Training

A bachelor's degree in agriculture or soil science is the minimum educational requirement to become a soil scientist. Typical courses include physics, geology, bacteriology, botany, chemistry, soil and plant morphology, soil fertility, soil classification, and soil genesis.

Research and teaching positions usually require higher levels of education. Most colleges of agriculture also offer master's and doctoral degrees. In addition to studying agriculture or soil science, students can specialize in biology, chemistry, physics, or engineering.

Certification or Licensing

Though not required, many soil scientists may seek certification to enhance their careers. The American Society of Agronomy and the Soil Science Society of America offer certification in the following areas: crop advisory, agronomy, and soil science/classification. In order to be accepted into a program, applicants must meet certain levels of education and experience.

The U.S. Department of Labor (DOL) reports that some states require soil scientists to be licensed. Typical licensing requirements include having a "bachelor's degree with a certain number of credit hours in soil science, a certain number of years working under a licensed scientist, and passage of an examination."

Other Requirements

Soil scientists must be able to work effectively both on their own and with others on projects, either outdoors or in the lab.

Technology is increasingly used in this profession; an understanding of word processing, the Internet, multimedia software, databases, and even computer programming can be useful. Soil scientists spend many hours outdoors in all kinds of weather, so they must be able to endure sometimes difficult and uncomfortable physical conditions. They must be detail oriented to do accurate research, and they should enjoy solving puzzles—figuring out, for example, why a crop isn't flourishing and what fertilizers should be used.

EXPLORING

The National FFA Organization can introduce you to the concerns of farmers and researchers. Joining a 4-H club can also give you valuable experience in agriculture. Contact the local branch of these organizations, your county's soil conservation department, or other government agencies to learn about regional projects. If you live in an agricultural community, you may be able to find opportunities for part-time or summer work on a farm or ranch.

EMPLOYERS

Approximately 14,000 soil and plant scientists are employed in the United States. Most soil scientists work for state or federal departments of agriculture. However, they may also work for other public employers, such as land appraisal boards, land-grant colleges and universities, and conservation departments. Soil scientists who work overseas may be employed by the U.S. Agency for International Development.

Soil scientists are needed in private industries as well, such as agricultural service companies, banks, insurance and real estate firms, food products companies, wholesale distributors, and environmental and engineering consulting groups. Private firms may hire soil scientists for sales or research positions.

STARTING OUT

In the public sector, college graduates can apply directly to the Natural Resources Conservation Service of the Department of Agriculture, the Department of the Interior, the Environmental Protection Agency, or other state government agencies for beginning positions. University career services offices generally have listings for these openings as well as opportunities available in private industry.

ADVANCEMENT

Salary increases are the most common form of advancement for soil scientists. The nature of the job may not change appreciably even after many years of service. Higher administrative and supervisory positions are few in comparison with the number of jobs that must be done in the field.

Opportunities for advancement will be higher for those with advanced degrees. For soil scientists engaged in teaching, advancement may translate into a higher academic rank with more responsibility. In private business firms, soil scientists have opportunities to advance into positions such as department head or research director. Supervisory and manager positions are also available in state agencies such as road or conservation departments.

EARNINGS

According to the DOL, median annual earnings in 2009 for soil and plant scientists were $59,180. The lowest paid 10 percent earned less than $34,930; the middle 50 percent earned between $45,070 and $78,590; and the highest paid 10 percent made more than $107,670.

Federal mean salaries for soil scientists were higher; in 2009, they made $78,250 a year. Government earnings depend in large part on levels of experience and education. Those with doctorates and a great deal of experience may qualify for higher government positions, with salaries ranging from $80,000 to $120,000. Other than short-term research projects, most jobs offer health and retirement benefits in addition to an annual salary.

WORK ENVIRONMENT

Most soil scientists work 40 hours a week. Their job is varied, ranging from fieldwork collecting samples, to labwork analyzing their findings. Some jobs may involve travel, even to foreign countries. Other positions may include teaching or supervisory responsibilities for field training programs.

OUTLOOK

The *Occupational Outlook Handbook* reports that employment within the field of soil science is expected to grow faster than the average for all occupations through 2018. Soil scientists will be needed to help create more food for our growing population, develop plans to fight erosion and other types of soil degradation, and help developers comply with environmental regulations.

The career of soil scientist is affected by the government's involvement in farming studies; as a result, budget cuts at the federal and (especially) state levels may limit funding for this type of job. However, private businesses will continue to demand soil scientists for research and sales positions. Companies dealing with seed, fertilizers, or farm equipment are examples of private employers that hire soil scientists.

Technological advances in equipment and methods of conservation will allow scientists to better protect the environment, as well as improve farm production. Scientists' ability to evaluate soils and plants will improve with more precise research methods. Combine-mounted yield monitors will produce data as the farmer crosses the field, and satellites will provide more detailed field information. With computer images, scientists will also be able to examine plant roots more carefully.

A continued challenge facing future soil scientists will be convincing farmers to change their current methods of tilling and chemical treatment in favor of environmentally safer methods. They must encourage farmers to balance increased agricultural output with the protection of our limited natural resources.

FOR MORE INFORMATION

The ASA has information on careers, certification, and college chapters. For details, contact
American Society of Agronomy (ASA)
5585 Guilford Road
Madison, WI 53711-5801
Tel: 608-273-8080
https://www.agronomy.org

For information on seminars, issues affecting soil scientists, and educational institutions offering soil science programs, contact
National Society of Consulting Soil Scientists
PO Box 1219
Sandpoint, ID 83864-0860
Tel: 800-535-7148
http://www.nscss.org

Contact the NRCS for information on government soil conservation careers. Its Web site has information on volunteer opportunities.

Natural Resources Conservation Service (NRCS)
U.S. Department of Agriculture
1400 Independence Avenue, SW
Washington, DC 20250-0002
http://www.nrcs.usda.gov

For information on soil conservation, college student chapters, and publications, contact
Soil and Water Conservation Society
945 SW Ankeny Road
Ankeny, IA 50023-9723
Tel: 515-289-2331
http://www.swcs.org

For information on certification and the career brochure Soils Sustain Life, *contact*
Soil Science Society of America
5585 Guilford Road
Madison, WI 53711-5801
Tel: 608-273-8080
https://www.soils.org

Index

Entries and page numbers in **bold** indicate major treatment of a topic.